An ex-IT consultant turned livestock farmer and always a keen cook, Jackie has been barbecuing for more than 35 years. She became an ambassador of the 'low-and-slow' method of barbecue in the UK after taking a competition barbecue class in the USA in May 2003. In October 2004, she became the first and to date only non-American to win the coveted 'Grand Champion' Title at the Jack Daniel's Invitational BBQ Competition in Lynchburg, Tennessee.

Jackie owns and runs BBQ Workshop, an independent barbecue cookery school in Kent; she also produces her own range of award-winning rubs and spice blends. Jackie also runs a restaurant consultancy business combining her knowledge and experience of low-and-slow barbecue cooking, outside catering, meat production and barbecue equipment to assist the setup of new restaurants. She has worked with celebrity chefs, top chefs and complete beginners, introducing them to low-and-slow cooking over wood. One of the early pioneers of bringing American-style barbecue to the UK, she is proud to have been heavily involved with several very successful restaurants and is looking forward to passing on her knowledge and experience to many more, helping to bring the American style of low-and-slow barbecue into the UK.

JACKIE WEIGHT

A KISS OF SMOKE

AUSTIN MACAULEY PUBLISHERS™

LONDON • CAMBRIDGE • NEW YORK • SHARJAH

A CIP catalogue record for this title is available from the British Library.

ISBN 9781398485563 (Paperback)
ISBN 9781398485570 (Hardback)
ISBN 9781398485587 (ePub e-book)

www.austinmacauley.com

First Published 2023
Austin Macauley Publishers Ltd˚
1 Canada Square
Canary Wharf
London
E14 5AA

For my late husband, Rick Weight, the man who introduced me to so many great things, including farming and American-style barbecue. You swept me off my feet and showed me the world; without you, I wouldn't be the person I am today.

To Dave Hughes, thank you for putting up with me and my sometimes-strange recipes, for eating and critiquing my finished dishes, and remembering to take photos of the food before diving in. But mainly for loving me, challenging me and encouraging me.

I'd like to acknowledge and thank the following people for their support over the years.

To Ray Lampe, aka Dr BBQ, for introducing me to American-style barbecue.

To Cookshack and Fast Eddy's – Ed Maurin and his wife, Kathy, for driving across America to loan us their barbecues so that we could compete.

To Drew, Becky and Jennifer Grega for being there to support us whether we won or not.

To Nick and Darren at The American BBQ Company and the McKend family of ProQ Smokers for sending us barbecues to use in creating some of the recipes in this book.

To all of the wonderful people who have been to our barbecue workshops, it's been a pleasure meeting you and showing you how to improve your barbecue skills; we look forward to continuing to teach the art of barbecuing to as many people as possible. To join our barbecue family, you can find more information about our school at www.bbqworkshop.co.uk.

Contents

INTRODUCTION

First of all, if you're reading this, then thank you for having my book on your bookshelf: it's been a while in the making. I thought it might be nice to start with my story.

I've had a pretty diverse past. I started my career fresh from secretarial college to a first job in a typing pool and gradually worked my way up into the world of information technology, culminating in many years spent working in the City of London for financial institutions as an IT operations manager. I've been lucky enough to travel throughout Europe, Asia, America and as far as New Zealand; I spent my honeymoon Cattle Ranching in Canada; I even spent three years in the Territorial Army. However, in early 2002, I gave up my City life in favour of running our small farm. I found myself looking after and breeding over 250 head of cattle, pigs and a menagerie of chickens, ducks, guinea fowl,

peacocks and geese. Memories of getting up in the small hours in dressing gown and wellies to calve a cow and welcome her new calf into the world will always stay with me, as will showing cattle at Agricultural Shows, sometimes with great success, others with me being dragged through the mud holding on to a somewhat excited, wayward bull!

Through everything, my love of food has always been there, from cooking to baking and eventually to barbecue. My love of low-and-slow American-style barbecue started early by UK standards, and to be honest, somewhat reluctantly. It all began with a 'big' birthday which, according to my late husband Rick, called for a big birthday present…a road trip to America. Flying into Atlanta, stopping by some interesting sights along the way – who knew that Chattanooga really does have a Choo Choo? – and seeing some of the wonderful places America has to offer. We arrived in Lynchburg, Tennessee, a few days later to our intended destination – a Barbecue Cooking School… This was very new to me: I'm not really sure I was terribly interested in spending my birthday this way before I got there, but once I met the other guys on the class, I realised that it looked like it was going to be fun. The cook school was run by Ray Lampe, aka Dr BBQ. His reputation in barbecue circles was and still is right up there: he was very deservedly inducted into the Barbecue Hall of Fame a few years ago. (Yes, there really is such a thing)!

putting things into practice. I spent hours with my local butcher trying to describe the cuts of meat that I wanted. He'd never heard of a 'Boston butt' or a 'packer cut' of brisket, but between us we finally got what we were looking for.

Between running my farm, breeding and showing my cattle and pigs, I started a new venture of food production and outside catering: making home-cured bacon, sausages, smoked foods and cooking low-and-slow American-style barbecue at events and parties… It was slow to catch on – people still saw barbecue as burgers and sausages – but I persevered, and soon people were asking me to cook this new style of barbecue at functions and weddings. I'd like to think I was one of the early pioneers of barbecue in the UK. However, I draw the line at being called the 'Grandmother' of the UK barbecue scene… in fact, that title earned its author a sharp slap!

Needless to say, I became hooked on this 'new' style of barbecue and having spent a very memorable few days in Lynchburg, we continued our trip with a tour of as many little barbecue joints as we could find. The seed was planted. I took all my newfound knowledge home and bought a Weber Smoky Mountain Cooker, and started

My passion continued, and I was lucky enough to be invited to cook at the Jack Daniel's Invitational Barbecue World Championships later that year, I was thrilled and terrified at the same time. I'd never competed in a barbecue competition; heck, I'd never competed in any sort of cooking competition! With this, my barbecue Team 'Mad Cows' BBQ' was born with me at the helm as Chief Cook and Rick as my glamorous assistant!

October finally arrived, and after months of practice at home, we set off to Lynchburg. We cooked on a huge beast of a wood-burning smoker called a Jed Master, kindly loaned to us by a lovely guy who I had met at the barbecue class earlier that year, Drew 'Blindog' Grega; he and his friend Carl showed us how it worked. All I could think was how massive this beast was! We learnt a great lesson at The Jack: that competing was about doing your best and having fun. We did our best and came halfway through the pack but did not get our name called for any of the top 10 awards. However, we had a heck of a lot of fun, made some lifelong friends and survived through the experience of a lifetime.

Back home and continuing to cook, The American BBQ Company was born. We started importing American-style smokers to the UK, still in its infancy. A lot of time was spent on the road demonstrating, feeding people and selling Fast Eddy, Cookshack and Traeger Smokers to the public and caterers alike. The following spring, the lovely people at Jack Daniel's invited us to compete again, and of course we jumped at the chance. I had spent a lot of time practising on my Fast Eddy Pellet Cooker at the farm and asked Cookshack if they had one that I could borrow to cook on at The Jack, a request which they more than generously agreed to.

October came again, and off to Lynchburg we went, absolutely dumbfounded when Fast Eddy himself turned up with his cooking rig and the biggest Fast Eddy Smoker I've ever seen. He showed us how it worked, told us to help ourselves to anything in his catering kitchen and left us to it.

Well, I cooked my heart out that year but was totally amazed when our name was called for a third place in Pork. We took our place on the stage, received our prize and left to celebrate. When our name was called again with a top 10 in Brisket, we were ecstatic; I can't even describe how I felt when we were called again with a top 10 in Chicken, let alone when our name was called as International Grand Champion. Life was complete! We went off to celebrate with our new barbecue friends. We were having a wonderful time when suddenly one of the organisers came to find us to say, 'Haven't you heard your name being called'? To which we said, yes, we won the International section...to be told no, 'You've won the whole thing, you are the Grand Champions, they've called your name three times now, so please go up on stage and collect your prize!'

That was one of the best and most surprising moments of my life and a memory I shall always cherish.

Winning the Jack came with entries to some amazing barbecue competitions across the US, and we had the honour of competing at The Houston Livestock Show and Rodeo - The American Royal. We've also cooked in quite a few smaller competitions around the US, and have been lucky enough to get a few prize calls.

My story started a while ago and I've been lucky enough to visit, cook and eat barbecue across America, from New York, through the Carolinas, Alabama, Tennessee, Georgia, Florida, Kansas, Missouri, Oklahoma and Texas over to California and up to Oregon. I've promoted the low-and-slow style of barbecue throughout the UK and into Europe; I've helped several new ventures become successful restaurants, and I've enjoyed every single minute of it.

In October 2007 I lost my husband and cohort Rick to pancreatic cancer, after a final year together, filled with bouts of chemo, travel (including one final barbecue competition in Huntsville, Alabama), laughter, tears and great memories.

In December 2009, I met the 'new' man in my life, Dave. I was lucky to find someone who would encourage my passion for barbecue and cooking to continue.

In 2013, I was invited back to The Jack to compete in 'The Winners' Circle', a champion-of-champion cook-off between 25 years of Jack Daniel's champions. It was great to be able to take Dave with me, so that he could finally see what all the fun of a barbecue competition was about. After eight years of not competing, I was pretty happy to get second place in Brisket. It was great fun meeting all of my 'barbecue family' again.

Barbecue is still a big part of my life, even now. I have released my own range of rubs and spice mixes. I also run a successful barbecue cookery school in Kent, alongside my restaurant consultancy business. I love to spread the knowledge of barbecue at all levels.

This book is some of my story in food: not always traditional American-style barbecue, but things I've tasted on my travels and adapted for the barbecue and others that don't go near a barbecue but go so well with the style of cooking. Also, I couldn't miss the chance to put my passion for baking into print. Heck, I could spend my life in my kitchen and as long as I have people to feed, will always be happy.

The photos we have taken for this book are of real food which was cooked, photographed and eaten: no filters, no fakery, just plain home cooking. Extra thanks to my other half, Dave, for his constant nagging to finish this book his help with the photography – and of course his appetite!

FROM THE BARK TO THE SAUCE

Rubs

With all of the rubs, simply put the ingredients into a container and mix well.

Kansas City Rub

125 g brown sugar
65 g smoked paprika
1 tablespoon black pepper
1 tablespoon salt
1 tablespoon chilli powder
1 tablespoon garlic powder
1 tablespoon onion powder
1 teaspoon cayenne powder

Basic Pork Rub

100 g demerara sugar
70 g sweet paprika
15 g ground black pepper
15 g salt
15 g chilli powder
15 g garlic granules
15 g onion powder
5 g cayenne powder

Carolina Barbecue Rub

65 g smoked paprika
2 tablespoons salt
2 tablespoons white sugar
2 tablespoons brown sugar
1 tablespoon chilli powder
1 tablespoon black pepper
1 tablespoon ground cumin
1 tablespoon cayenne pepper

Mocha Rub

2 tablespoons sea salt
2 tablespoons coarse black pepper
2 tablespoons cocoa powder
2 tablespoons ground coffee
1 teaspoon coriander
1 teaspoon cinnamon
1 teaspoon chipotle chilli powder
8 juniper berries – crushed

Cajun Rub

2 teaspoons ground black pepper
2 teaspoons celery seed
6 teaspoons paprika
2 teaspoons cayenne powder
1½ teaspoons ground thyme
1½ teaspoons ground oregano
2 teaspoons dried mustard
2 teaspoons onion powder
2 teaspoons garlic granules
3 teaspoons brown sugar
3 teaspoons salt
2 teaspoons ground turmeric

Memphis Style Rub

75 g sweet paprika
2 tablespoons onion powder
2 tablespoons black pepper
2 tablespoons salt
1 tablespoon garlic granules
1 tablespoon cayenne

Jerk Rub

150 g ground allspice
150 g lemon pepper
150 g dark brown sugar
75 g onion powder
50 g garlic granules
50 g dried thyme
50 g salt
50 g ground chipotle chilli
25 g cinnamon
25 g ground nutmeg

Basic Dukkah

I lived in Sharm el Sheikh, Egypt for a little while and whilst I was there, I discovered Dukkah. Simply served by dipping flatbread into olive oil or local labneh and then into the Dukkah, it was a revelation! I branched out a little after that and tried using it as a crust on meat and discovered it was a very versatile mix!

110 g roasted almonds

80 g toasted sesame seeds

2 tablespoons coriander seeds – crushed

2 tablespoons cumin seeds – crushed

2 teaspoons freshly ground black pepper

1 teaspoon flaked sea salt

Place all ingredients into a blender and pulse until combined.

Store in a jar, close with a lid and store in the fridge.

This works well as a crust on chicken and firm fish, such as cod or hake.

Luxury Dukkah

When you want to push the boat out a bit, this makes an amazing flavour coating – or just eat it straight from the jar.

150 g roasted macadamia nuts

150 g roasted almonds

50 g toasted sesame seeds

2 teaspoons turmeric

1 teaspoon ground cumin

1 teaspoon freshly ground black pepper

½ teaspoon salt

½ teaspoon ground cinnamon

½ teaspoon ground ginger

Place macadamia nuts into a blender. Pulse no more than three or four times, or you will end up with an oily mess. Pour into a bowl.

Place the remaining ingredients into the blender and pulse until mixed and the almonds have been chopped up.

Mix into the bowl with the macadamia nuts.

Store in a jar, close with a lid and refrigerate until needed.

This makes a good rust on lamb and chicken. It also makes a good filling when stuffing into meats: see Dukkah Stuffed Lamb later in the book.

Sauces

Sweet Carolina Sauce

The acidic sweetness of this sauce helps cut through the richness of pulled pork. The sauce should be made at least 24 hours before using, to allow the acidity to mellow.

250 g yellow American-style mustard

150 g caster sugar

100 ml cider vinegar

5 g ground black pepper

3 g fine sea salt

60 g butter – cubed

Mix all ingredients, except the butter, in a saucepan. Bring to the boil and simmer gently for no more than 5 minutes. Remove from the heat and whisk in the cubed butter. Refrigerate overnight to allow flavours to mellow. Keep in the fridge and use within one month.

Buffalo Wing Sauce

This uses the same base sauce as the Sweet Carolina sauce with the addition of Frank's RedHot sauce.

1 batch Sweet Carolina Sauce *(as above)*

200 g Frank's RedHot sauce

Make a batch of Sweet Carolina sauce (as recipe above). Whilst still hot, but off the heat, whisk in the Frank's RedHot sauce to finish. (Add more for a hotter sauce, less for a milder sauce.)

Alabama White Sauce

This sauce is wonderful on smoked turkey and chicken.

180 g mayonnaise

60 ml cider vinegar

40 ml lemon juice

40 ml apple juice

1 tablespoon sugar

1 tablespoon garlic granules

1 tablespoon horseradish sauce

1 tablespoon cracked black pepper

½ teaspoon salt

Zest of one lemon – finely grated

½ teaspoon cayenne pepper

Blend all the ingredients together until fully combined and lump-free. Refrigerate for at least two hours before use to allow the flavours to mellow.

Refrigerate and use within one month.

Korean BBQ Glaze

Korean Barbecue is becoming more popular in the UK. This glaze gives a great flavour.

250 g light brown sugar	2 cloves garlic – crushed
250 ml light soy sauce	4 cm piece of ginger – finely grated
50 ml water	1 teaspoon sesame oil
1 tablespoon Gochujang paste	1 tablespoon toasted sesame seeds
1 tablespoon Shaoxing rice wine	1 teaspoon cornflour

Mix all ingredients, except sesame oil, sesame seeds and cornflour, in a saucepan. Bring to the boil and simmer gently for five minutes.

Make a 'slurry' of cornflour and a tablespoon of water. Whisk it into the sauce with the sesame oil and seeds and bring back to the boil to thicken.

Refrigerate overnight to allow the flavours to mellow. Keep in the fridge and use within one month.

Cherry Bourbon BBQ Sauce

This seems to be everyone's favourite sauce! I wasn't sure if I was going to put this recipe in the book, but so many people have asked me for it that I decided it was time to share.

1 kg frozen dark cherries – pitted	1 tablespoon onion granules
450 g tomato ketchup *(see Tip below)*	1 tablespoon garlic granules
100 ml Bourbon whiskey	2 teaspoons ground black pepper
70 ml cider vinegar	1 teaspoon orange zest – grated
70 ml soy sauce	1 teaspoon cinnamon
70 g sugar	50 g butter – cubed
35 ml Worcestershire sauce	

Add all of the ingredients into a saucepan (except the butter), mix well (whisk). Bring to a boil and then reduce the heat to a simmer.

Simmer the sauce until thickened, stirring regularly: this should take approximately 30 minutes. Remove from the heat and add the butter.

Using a stick blender, blend until smooth. Pass the sauce through a sieve to remove any cherry stones or lumps.

> TIP: When using tomato ketchup in a sauce, it's best not to use the most well-known brand, but to use a cheaper one which has a less dominant flavour of tomato.

'Dr Pepper' Barbecue Sauce

The lovely flavours of Dr Pepper are heightened in this sweet sticky sauce. It's a perfect foil for ribs and beef. This also works well with Cherry Cola!

1 litre Dr Pepper

250 ml tomato ketchup

2 tablespoons cider vinegar

2 tablespoons soy sauce

1 tablespoon Worcestershire sauce

1 teaspoon onion powder

1 teaspoon garlic granules

1 teaspoon ground black pepper

1 teaspoon fresh orange zest

50 g butter

In a saucepan, boil the Dr Pepper and reduce until only 250 ml of it remains. Add the remaining ingredients (except the butter), mix well and bring to a simmer. Cook for 30–40 minutes, stirring often, until thickened. Remove from the heat, add the butter and blend until smooth. Refrigerate and use within 1 month.

Spicy Peanut Butter & Jelly Sauce

Great on Chicken Wings and Pork Ribs.

1 red onion – grated

4 cloves garlic – crushed

500 g crunchy peanut butter

500 g strawberry jam

100 g Worcestershire sauce

100 g sriracha

25 g fish sauce

Water *(to loosen sauce if it is too thick)*

Fry the onions and garlic until soft; blend them if they are not really finely chopped.

Place all the ingredients into a pan and bring to the boil; add water to loosen the sauce if necessary. Remove from the heat and allow to cool.

Kansas Ketchup

A great tomato-based sauce on its own, but you can use it as a base and add your own choice of fruit, herbs or spices to customise.

60 g sunflower oil

1 medium onion – finely chopped

2 cloves of fresh garlic

1 teaspoon celery seed

1 teaspoon chipotle chilli – ground

500 ml tomato ketchup

50 g tomato purée

50 ml cider vinegar

50 g brown sugar

35 g yellow mustard

40 ml apple juice

20 ml soy sauce

20 ml Worcestershire sauce

Salt and pepper to taste

In a saucepan over medium heat, add the oil, onion, garlic and chipotle chilli. Cook, stirring occasionally, until soft. Add the remaining ingredients, mix well and bring to a simmer. Simmer for approximately 30 minutes, stirring often, until thickened. Remove from heat and blend with a stick blender until smooth. If you're going to use as a table sauce, pass through a sieve.

A KISS OF SMOKE

Basic Hot Sauce

There's a definite kick to this one. Best to make it in a well-ventilated room – we don't want you succumbing to those chilli fumes!

300 g tomato ketchup	50 ml agave nectar
200 ml water	1 medium onion – chopped
250 g Scotch bonnet chilli	3 cloves of garlic – crushed
250 g Habanero chilli	50 g butter
100 ml cider vinegar	
50 g Scorpion chilli	

Smoke chopped onion, chillies and garlic at a low temperature for one hour. Place the smoked onion, chillies and garlic in a pan and fry gently until soft. Add the other ingredients, except the butter and bring to the boil. Simmer for around an hour. Remove from the heat and add the butter, blend. Pass through a sieve if you want a smooth sauce.

Chilli Jam

1 large onion	500 g granulated sugar
20 ml sunflower oil	500 ml cider or red wine vinegar
10 fresh red chillies	3 Scotch bonnet chillies
3 roasted red peppers	1 teaspoon sea salt
4 cloves garlic	

Remove the skin from the roasted red peppers (you can use the ones in jars if you prefer).

Chop the onion and fry in a little sunflower oil until soft.

Put the chillies, onions, garlic and red peppers into a blender and pulse until finely chopped (don't purée them).

Place the chopped chilli mixture into a pan, add the sugar and vinegar. Bring to the boil.

Prick the Scotch bonnets with the point of a knife and add to the pan with the salt.

Soft-boil until the jam is reduced by around half and is quite thick and glossy.

Pour into sterilised jars, add one scotch bonnet to each jar (or remove if you don't want it too hot).

Seal jars and leave for at least one week to mellow before using.

Fiery Mango Sauce

I always used to find difficult to develop new hot sauces as I was a total chilli wimp! However, in my advanced years I've grown to love chilli heat and really enjoy something with a good kick!

200 g onions – finely chopped	200 g cider vinegar
10 ml vegetable oil	100 g brown sugar
25 g tomato paste	3 Scotch bonnet chillies
400 g tinned tomatoes	10 g sea salt
300 g tinned mango pulp	3 cloves garlic
	3 g ground black pepper

Fry the onion in the oil until soft. Add the remaining ingredients into a pan and bring to the boil. Reduce to a simmer and cook for a further 15 minutes – check the seasoning, then remove from the heat.

Add 50 g cubed butter and use a stick blender to make a smooth emulsion.

Burger Sauce/Dirty Mayo

300 g mayonnaise	1 teaspoon cayenne pepper
100 g tomato ketchup	1 teaspoon smoked paprika
75 g Dijon mustard	1 teaspoon sugar
50 g gherkins – finely chopped	Pinch each of salt and pepper
20 ml cider vinegar	
2 garlic cloves – finely grated	

Mix all ingredients for the burger sauce and set aside in the fridge until ready to use.

Pickles and Relishes

Smoked Beetroot Relish

700 g beetroot – peeled and cut into eighths

250 g onions – peeled and cut into eighths

100 g sugar

100 ml water

100 ml red wine vinegar

40 g grated horseradish

10 g brown mustard seeds

1 teaspoon salt

Place onions and beetroot into a shallow dish and place in the smoker. Smoke for approximately 1 hour at 100°C.

Place beetroot and onions into a food blender and pulse, pushing down the sides every 10 seconds to incorporate all the beet and to check on size. The resulting pieces should be similar in size to lentils.

Place in a pan with sugar, water, horseradish, mustard seeds, vinegar and salt and simmer for 15–20 minutes. The beetroot should be cooked, but not soft and mushy.

May be stored in the fridge for a week, or you can place in sterilised jars and seal to keep longer.

Beetroot Pickled Eggs

I keep a few chickens and guinea fowl out in my paddock so always have lots of eggs around. These pickled eggs are great on their own (in a bag of crisps) or chopped up in a salad.

8 eggs

1 jar pickled baby beetroot

125 ml red wine vinegar

125 ml white distilled vinegar

2 tablespoons light brown sugar

1 teaspoon sea salt

Place eggs in a saucepan and cover with water (so that the eggs are just covered). Bring to the boil and cook for 5 minutes. Remove from the heat and place under cold running water to stop them cooking. Peel and set aside.

Place the water, vinegars, the liquid from the jar of beetroot pickle, sugar and salt together in a pan and bring to the boil. Place the pickled beetroot and eggs into a large jar, alternating them as much as possible. Pour in the hot liquid, carefully knock out any air bubbles and seal the jar. Leave to cool.

Let the pickles mature for at least 48 hours before eating. Once opened, keep in the fridge.

Smoked Cranberry Bourbon Relish

This goes wonderfully with smoked turkey.

500 g fresh or frozen cranberries

175 g caster sugar

½ teaspoon ground cinnamon

1 fresh orange – zested and sliced

50 ml Bourbon Whiskey

Put the cranberries in a large ovenproof dish, sprinkle the sugar over them, along with the cinnamon and the grated zest of the orange. Slice the orange and place over the cranberries.

Put into the barbecue at 110°C for one hour, or until the cranberries are soft.

Remove from smoker, cool a little and squeeze the juice from the orange slices. Mash the cranberries with a fork until all have 'popped'.

Add the Bourbon. Mix well and return to the smoker for a further 30 minutes.

Serve hot or cold.

Lime Pickled Cauliflower

Tart, crunchy and savoury – a great snack, lovely with smoked meat and cheese!

1 head of cauliflower	½ teaspoon coriander seeds
350 ml cider vinegar	
2 teaspoons salt	½ teaspoon black peppercorns
1 lime – sliced	

Wash cauliflower and break into florets. In a large saucepan, add the cider vinegar and salt and bring to the boil. Add the cauliflower florets, coriander and peppercorns, stir, bring back to the boil and remove from the heat.

Place half of the lime slices into the bottom of a large jar then pack the cauliflower florets on top before topping with the final half of the lime slices. Pour the pickling liquid over the mix until the jar is full – make sure the seeds are in the jar. Seal the jar with its lid and leave to cool. Once cool, refrigerate for at least 24 hours before eating – the more time you can give them, the better they will be.

Quick Pickled Radishes

Radishes have to be one of the easiest crops to grow, even in a small garden. I like to use red wine vinegar for this pickle, as it gives the radishes a lovely rosy hue.

12 radishes – washed	1 teaspoon sea salt
125 ml red wine vinegar	3 juniper berries – lightly crushed
125 ml water	
1 tablespoon caster sugar	

Top and tail the radishes and slice them as thinly as possible before packing them into a jar with the juniper berries.

Mix the water, vinegar, sugar and salt together until the sugar and salt have dissolved. Pour the mixture over the radishes, ensuring they are covered.

Seal the jar and refrigerate for 30 minutes before serving.

Shallots Pickled in Balsamic Vinegar

I've been making these for years; they're crisp and crunchy, and the balsamic vinegar gives them that hint of sweetness without the need for sugar.

1 kg small shallots	500 ml balsamic vinegar
200 g salt	

Peel the shallots. Place in a large shallow dish and sprinkle with salt. Leave for 24 hours, tossing them occasionally – the salt helps to remove excess moisture, giving you a crunchier pickle. Rinse the shallots thoroughly and leave to dry. Pack into sterilised jars and pour the balsamic vinegar over the shallots until the jar is filled. Seal jar and leave in a dark cupboard for at least one month before eating.

Dressings and Chutneys

Strawberry Balsamic Dressing

500 ml balsamic vinegar   250 ml litre olive oil

200 g strawberry jam

Place balsamic vinegar and jam into a pan. Bring to the boil and reduce until only about half remains. Leave to cool.

Add the oil. Using a stick blender, blend the mixture to form an emulsion. Decant into a squeeze bottle and use within six months.

VARIATION:

This also works well with raspberry jam or any berry jelly.

Blue Cheese Dressing

200 g blue cheese *(like Stilton)* – crumbled

200 g mayonnaise

50 g cider vinegar

50 g sour cream

1 tablespoon sugar

Blend all ingredients together. Leave in the fridge for 24 hours before using.

Maid of Kent Chutneys

I used to have a little business selling preserves, sausages and bacon called Maid of Kent. Here are a few of my favourite award-winning chutney recipes.

Pink Pear and Ginger Chutney

1.4 kg conference pears – peeled, cored and chopped

225 g onions – peeled and chopped

50 g stem ginger – finely chopped

Grated rind and juice of 1 orange

25 g root ginger – roughly chopped

3 whole cloves

350 g granulated sugar

350 ml red wine vinegar

Tie the root ginger and cloves into a muslin bag and place all the ingredients into a large pan.

Stir over a low heat until the sugar dissolves.

Bring to the boil, reduce the heat and simmer for 1½ hours or until the chutney is thick.

Remove muslin bag and while still hot ladle into hot sterile jars. Seal with airtight, vinegar-proof covers. Leave to mature for a month before using.

Haymakers Chutney

1 kg red tomatoes

350 g light soft brown sugar

225 ml cider vinegar

225 ml Balsamic Vinegar

250 g desert apples

250 g sweet red peppers

250 g onions

175 g raisins

175 g sultanas

3 cloves garlic

2 red chillies

1 teaspoon ground ginger

1 teaspoon ground allspice

1 teaspoon mustard powder

2 teaspoons salt

Peel and chop tomatoes and apples. Finely chop onions and peppers. Mince garlic and chillies. Put all ingredients into preserving pan, bring to boil then simmer until chutney is has thickened.

Ladle into sterilised jars and mature for at least one month before serving.

Mango Chutney

700 g mangoes – peeled, de-stoned and diced into 1 cm cubes	1 teaspoon hot chilli powder
225 g sugar	2 inch piece cinnamon stick
230 ml white vinegar	50 g raisins
25 g root ginger – peeled and finely chopped	50 g dates – chopped
3 cloves of garlic – crushed	2 cardamom pods (seeds only)

Place the sugar and vinegar into a pan and bring to the boil. When the sugar has dissolved, add the remaining ingredients and bring the mixture back to the boil, stirring occasionally.

Reduce the heat and simmer the chutney, stirring frequently, until it is thick. Discard the cinnamon stick. Spoon while still hot into hot prepared jars. Seal with airtight, vinegar-proof covers.

Bacon and Red Onion Jam

Two magic words, bacon and jam...what could be better? Bourbon, that's what!

500 g thick smoked streaky bacon – cut into 1 cm pieces	75 ml cider vinegar
3 large red onions – thinly sliced	75 g brown sugar
4 cloves garlic – chopped	75 ml maple syrup
	75 ml Bourbon whiskey
	1 teaspoon chipotle chilli paste

Cook the bacon in a large frying pan until the fat has rendered and the bacon starts to get crispy. Remove the bacon from the pan, leaving the fat and add the sliced onions. Fry until tender and starting to caramelise, then add the garlic and fry for another minute.

Add the vinegar to deglaze the pan, followed by the brown sugar, maple syrup, Bourbon, bacon and chipotle chilli paste. Reduce the heat and simmer until reduced to a syrupy consistency: about 1–2 hours.

Place the jam into a food processor and pulse a few times to bring the ingredients together. Do not purée it; you want a good chunky consistency. Serve or store it in a sealed container in the fridge for up to four weeks.

VARIATION:

You can use leftover cooked ham instead of bacon.

A Glut of Jalapenos!

What to do with all those jalapenos that you grew...the choices are endless, but these are my two favourite recipes

Pickled Jalapenos

20 fresh jalapenos – sliced into 3–5 mm rounds	100 ml water
	500 ml white vinegar
	100 g sea salt

Wash and sterilise some jars: you'll need around three jam jars for this recipe. Pack the sliced jalapenos into the jars, finishing around 1 cm from the top.

Put the vinegar, water and salt into a pan and bring to a rolling boil. Carefully ladle the hot liquid into the jars. Put the lid on each jar and close until finger-tight – don't over tighten them.

Water bath – Place the jars into a large saucepan with a cloth at the base and add hot water until the jars are submerged to just below the lid. Bring the water to the boil and simmer for around 15 minutes. Allow the jars to cool before removing from the water. The lids will make a 'popping' sound when the vacuum is formed inside the jar (this will happen during the cooling time). If the lid is firm, then the seal has worked and the jalapenos can be stored safely. If the lid has any movement, place these jars in the fridge and use within one month.

Cowboy Candies (Candied Jalapenos)

Sweet sticky jalapeños that work well with desserts and savoury dishes.

20 jalapenos – sliced into 3–5 mm rounds	1 teaspoon hot chilli powder
250 g white sugar	1 teaspoon ground turmeric
125 ml cider vinegar	1 inch piece of root ginger – grated

Place the sugar, vinegar, chilli, turmeric and ginger into a large pan and bring to the boil, stirring until the sugar has dissolved. Reduce the liquid until it gets to a syrup.

Add the jalapenos and simmer for around 5 minutes. Transfer into prepared jars (as in previous recipe) and top with the remaining syrup. (Any leftover syrup can be saved and used as a topping on ice cream or in a salad dressing.)

Use the water bath method as before, to complete the preserving process.

SIPS, STARTERS, SOUPS, SNACKS AND SIDES

Smoky Mary

Adding a little smoke to a traditional Bloody Mary perks up the flavour and paves the way for those smoky delights to follow.

4 parts tomato juice	*Garnish*
2 parts vodka	Old bay seasoning
Splash of Worcestershire sauce	Olives and pickled chillies
Sriracha to taste	Wedge of lime
Pinch of celery salt	
Ice – cubed or crushed	

Pour tomato juice into a shallow dish and place in smoker on a low setting for 30 minutes; chill.

Mix all the ingredients (except the garnish) together in a jug, half filled with ice. Stir well.

Dip rim of glass in lime juice and old bay seasoning.

Pour into glass and garnish with a lime wedge, olives and pickled chilli.

Espresso Martini

I discovered this on a visit to South Carolina and had to go back for more. It's not smoked but it goes down beautifully after a good barbecue!

1-part espresso coffee	1-part vanilla vodka
Vodka	Lemon rind
1-part Kahlua	

Rub the rim of the glass with lemon rind and leave the rind in the glass. Shake all the spirits over ice and pour into the glass over the lemon rind.

Corn Chowder

Rich, thick, warming and topped with bacon. It's a hug in a cup.

1 medium onion – finely diced

10 ml oil

250 g potatoes – cut into ½ cm dice

500 g frozen sweetcorn kernels

350 ml water

250 ml whole milk

100 ml double cream

Salt and pepper to taste

100 g streaky bacon, cooked until crisp.

Fry onion in olive oil until soft and translucent. Add diced potatoes and frozen corn, then cook for a further 10 minutes, stirring regularly. Add water, milk and cream, bring to the boil and simmer very gently until the potatoes have softened, but still retain a bit of bite.

Partially blend the soup with a stick blender... you want to retain some of the structure of the vegetables but blend to help thicken the soup and create different textures. Season with salt and black pepper to taste.

Serve topped with crumbled crispy bacon (optional) and some buttery toasted sourdough bread

Smoked Butternut Squash Soup

A smoky take on this classic favourite.

1 butternut squash – peeled and deseeded

850 ml hot vegetable stock

2 medium red onions – cut into eight wedges

4 tablespoons double cream, plus more to serve

2 tablespoons olive oil

2 mild red chillies – halved and deseeded

2 cloves of garlic

Salt and pepper

Fresh coriander

Cut the squash into large chunks, about 4 cm across, then toss in a large roasting tin with the onion wedges, garlic, chilli and half the olive oil. Place in a medium heat barbecue with maple wood and cook until tender. Tip the vegetables into a saucepan with the stock and simmer until all the vegetables are soft, add the cream, then blend with a stick blender until smooth. Return to the pan, gently reheat and season to taste.

Serve the soup in bowls with swirls of cream and chopped fresh coriander (optional), and with buttered sourdough toast on the side.

Clam Chowder

I fell in love with Clam chowder at 'Mo's' in Oregon. This is as close as I could get to the flavours I remember there. Mo's is still a firm favourite!

4 kg fresh clams – scrubbed and rinsed, opened clams discarded

8 rashers smoked streaky bacon – cut into 1 cm pieces

3 tablespoons butter

4 shallots – finely chopped

2 sticks celery – finely chopped

4 cloves garlic – finely chopped

4 sprigs fresh thyme leaves

2 bay leaves

2 large, peeled potatoes – cut into 1 cm cubes

To finish

250 ml double cream

¼ teaspoon freshly ground black pepper

Salt to taste

100 g cubed butter

3 tablespoons each of finely chopped fresh chives and flat leaf parsley

In a large stockpot, bring 500 ml of water to a boil. Add clams, cover and cook until most of the clams are opened. (Stir a few times.)

Transfer the clams to a bowl and strain the clam broth twice into a jug through a fine-mesh sieve lined with kitchen towel. Remove the clams from their shells. Discard the shells and put the cooking water to one side.

In a large saucepan, fry the bacon until crisp. Add the butter, onions and celery and cook until softened. Add the potatoes, garlic, thyme and bay leaves and cook until the vegetables are soft but still translucent.

Add the strained clam cooking water and bring to a boil. Lower the heat, cover and simmer for 20 to 30 minutes, or until the chowder thickens slightly and the potatoes are very tender. Use a potato masher to gently smash some of the potatoes: this will help to thicken the chowder.

Remove from the heat, stir in the clams, cubed butter and cream, season with salt and pepper. Cover and set aside for 1 hour to allow the flavours to mellow. When ready to serve, place the pot over low heat and gently reheat. Serve hot, sprinkled with parsley and chives with a big chunk of sourdough bread.

Note: you could use canned clams if you can't get fresh ones, in which case skip the first part of the instructions.

|||||||||||||||||||||||||||||||||||||||||||||||||||

Bourbon Sweet Potatoes

A firm favourite amongst friends and family, this rich, sweet yet savoury dish will make everyone come back for more.

1 kg sweet potatoes

100 g butter

50 ml Bourbon whiskey

1 teaspoon flaked sea salt

½ teaspoon ground cinnamon or mixed spice

Large pinch ground black pepper

Mini marshmallows or brown sugar *(optional)*

Bake the sweet potatoes until soft. (This can be done in a barbecue, oven or a microwave.)

Cut each potato in half, lengthwise and scoop out the flesh into a large bowl. Be careful not to damage the skins, as we will be serving the potato in the skins.

Mash the sweet potato flesh until smooth, add the remaining ingredients and mix thoroughly.

Spoon or pipe the mixture back into the potato skins and put into a barbecue or under a grill to heat through.

If you're feeling sweet-toothed, you can add mini-marshmallows or brown sugar on top before grilling.

Atomic Buffalo Turds!

Cook on the rack in the barbecue so that the filling is facing up, over indirect heat for 1 hour at 150°C, until the bacon is cooked through and nicely browned. Serve straight from the barbecue – they probably won't make it much further than that!

There's no disguising the real name of these rich, cheesy, bacon-covered pieces of deliciousness. Some call them jalapeno poppers but I call them by their real name!

200 g cream cheese

150 g grated cheese
(I like to use a blend of Cheddar, Red Leicester and mozzarella)

2 bird's eye chillies – very finely chopped

8 jalapeno chillies or mini sweet peppers

8 slices smoked streaky bacon

Mix the cream cheese with the grated cheeses and bird's eye chilli.

Halve the jalapenos (or mini sweet peppers) lengthwise: try to keep the stalk on each half. Using a teaspoon, scrape out the membrane and seeds.

Spoon (or pipe) some of the cream cheese filling into the halved jalapenos/mini peppers. Stretch out the streaky bacon on a board with a knife, cut in half and wrap it around the filled jalapeno/mini pepper. Repeat until all the jalapenos are covered with bacon. Ensure that the ends of the bacon finish underneath the pepper, so that they don't unravel when cooking.

Variation: For a vegetarian option, omit the bacon, mix some grated parmesan cheese and panko breadcrumbs together in a bowl and dip the cream cheese side of the chilli/ pepper into the crumb mix. Cook as above. This also works well using mushrooms instead of peppers.

Buttermilk Onion Bundles

A cross between onion rings and an onion bhaji, this fluffy bundle of onions will keep you coming back for more!

2 large white onions

Rapeseed oil for frying

200 ml buttermilk

100 g plain flour

10 g smoked paprika

1 teaspoon salt

1 teaspoon ground black pepper

½ teaspoon cayenne powder

Peel the onions cut in half and then cut crosswise (from root to top) into 4 mm thick slices. Separate slices into half rings. Coat the onion rings in buttermilk. Mix the remaining ingredients for the seasoned flour. Remove the onions from the buttermilk and shake off excess liquid then toss them into the seasoned flour mix until fully coated before shaking off excess flour. Leave for 5 minutes.

Heat the oil in a large deep fryer, to 180°C. Drop handfuls of onions into the deep fryer in a loose bundle form and fry until golden brown and crisp. Remove from the fryer, drain on kitchen paper and serve.

Devilish Piggies

These are a cross between pigs in blankets and devils on horseback – they're tasty!

Chipolatas (twisted into two mini sausages) or cocktail sausages

Semi-dried pitted prunes

Streaky bacon

Simply take a cocktail-sized sausage, lay it alongside a prune cut almost in half and elongated to the same size as the sausage then wrap in 'stretched' streaky bacon.

Cook over indirect heat on the barbecue for around one hour until fully cooked (internal temperature 75°C). These taste great hot or cold.

Frickles

The crisp coating followed by the crunch of the pickle make these a great side dish or snack – you can use any type of pickle for these, too!

175 g plain flour	½ teaspoon cayenne pepper
125 ml buttermilk	½ teaspoon garlic granules
25 g cornmeal	
1 egg	500 g dill pickles – either quartered lengthways or sliced ½ cm thick on the diagonal
½ tablespoon Worcestershire sauce	
½ teaspoon salt	
½ teaspoon ground black pepper	2 tablespoons flour for coating

In a large bowl, combine all of the batter ingredients and whisk together.

Preheat oil in a deep fryer to 180°C. Lightly coat the drained pickles with flour, dip them into the batter to coat and drop them into the fryer.

Deep fry until golden brown. Drain on paper towels. Add salt and pepper to taste.

Grilled Halloumi with Pea Guacamole

I love good-quality Halloumi. This makes a great starter or a meat free meal.

1 block halloumi cheese	Olive oil

Pea Guacamole

2 ripe avocados (*I use frozen avocado cubes for this dish too*)	4 semi-sundried tomatoes – finely chopped
200 g frozen peas – defrosted	Juice and finely grated zest of one lime
Small bunch fresh coriander – finely chopped	1 or 2 bird's eye chillies – finely chopped
	Salt and pepper to taste

Make the guacamole by placing the coriander, tomatoes, chillies and peas into a blender and blending until almost smooth. In a separate bowl, mash the avocados with the lime zest and juice and then mix in the blended ingredients. Season with salt and pepper to taste.

Slice the halloumi into 5 mm thick slices, brush with the olive oil and place onto a hot barbecue or a frying pan. Grill or fry until a crust is formed. Flip over and repeat on the other side.

Serve with toasted sourdough bread and salad.

American-Style Slaw

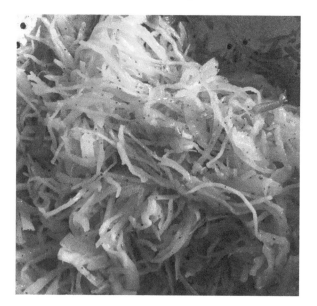

A tangy, sweet, mayonnaise-free slaw. Wonderful served with pulled pork or other 'rich' meats, as the acidity helps cut through the richness.

1 head white cabbage – finely shredded

2 red peppers – quartered and finely sliced

2 large carrots – grated

2 sticks celery – finely sliced

Dressing

250 ml sunflower oil

250 ml cider vinegar

150 g caster sugar

50 g tomato and chilli relish

2 tablespoons American mustard

1 teaspoon celery seeds

In a small saucepan combine the oil, sugar, vinegar and mustard. Bring to boil and boil for about 5 minutes until the sugar is dissolved. Stir in the relish and celery seed. Remove from heat and allow to cool.

In a large bowl, mix together the cabbage, pepper, carrot, celery, salt and pepper.

Pour the cooled dressing over the cabbage mixture and mix well. Cover and refrigerate for at least one hour. (The slaw tastes even better if made the day before to allow flavours to mellow.)

Mix again before serving.

Broccoli Slaw

I love this slaw, the addition of soft, chewy dried cranberries and cashew nuts adds texture and the sweet onion relish in the dressing really lifts it!

½ head white cabbage – finely shredded

2 carrots – grated

1 head broccoli – chopped into bite-sized pieces

100 g raw cashew nuts

100 g dried cranberries

Dressing

250 ml mayonnaise

100 ml sweet onion relish

25 g caster sugar

50 ml cider vinegar

1 teaspoon celery seeds

½ teaspoon black pepper

½ teaspoon salt

1 teaspoon mustard powder

In a large bowl, mix all of the dressing ingredients until fully combined. Add all of the prepared vegetables, fruit and nuts to the dressing and mix well until everything is coated.

Fennel and Apple Slaw

This is a fresh, tangy, mayonnaise-free slaw. It's great with pork, chicken and fish.

2 fennel bulbs

3 apples *(I used Pink Lady)*

½ head of white cabbage

Dressing

2 tablespoons wholegrain mustard

30 ml maple syrup

75 ml cider vinegar

75 ml olive oil

1 tablespoon fresh mint – chopped

fennel fronds – removed from the fennel bulbs and chopped

Add the dressing ingredients into a large bowl and whisk together until combined. Finely shred the fennel, apples and cabbage and put into the bowl. Mix into the dressing until everything is coated.

Red, White and Blue Slaw

This slaw is rich and creamy, bound together with a ranch-style dressing. It holds its own with barbecued beef dishes such as brisket and short ribs.

½ head white cabbage – shredded

½ head red cabbage – shredded

4 carrots – grated

4 sticks celery – finely sliced

Topping

200 g Stilton cheese – crumbled

200 g crispy bacon – crumbled

Dressing

250 g mayonnaise

75 g sour cream

75 g buttermilk

150 g cider vinegar

1 teaspoon parsley

1 teaspoon dill weed

½ teaspoon onion granules

½ teaspoon salt

½ teaspoon black pepper

2 tablespoons maple syrup

Mix the dressing ingredients together in a large bowl. Add the prepared vegetables and mix together until combined. Top with crumbled blue cheese and bacon, toss lightly.

Spiced Red Cabbage

This almost qualifies as a cooked slaw and can be served hot or cold with equal success.

1 tablespoon oil

1 head of red cabbage – quartered, cored and finely shredded

1 finger-size piece fresh root ginger – finely chopped

2 red onions – halved and thinly sliced

1 teaspoon ground allspice

Zest and juice of one orange – finely grated

500 g Bramley apples – chopped

50 g caster sugar

100 ml red wine vinegar

Heat oil in a large saucepan, add cabbage, ginger, onions, allspice and apple, then cook for five minutes until the cabbage is just starting to wilt. Scatter over the sugar and pour in the vinegar and orange zest.

Cover pan, gently cook for 10 minutes, then remove lid and turn up the heat to medium. Simmer the liquid in the cabbage for about 20 minutes, stirring occasionally, then stir continuously for the last few minutes until all the liquid has evaporated and the cabbage becomes sticky on the bottom of the pan.

Serve cabbage hot or cold.

Lynchburg Candied Apples

I have great memories of visiting Miss Mary Bobo's Boarding House in Lynchburg, Tennessee, on more than one occasion. Sitting around a big table with a group of strangers, eating wonderful home-cooked 'Southern' foods, washed down with sweet tea. The only alcohol allowed in the 'dry county' that houses the Jack Daniel's Distillery comes in the form of Miss Mary's Baked Apples – luscious apples stewed and steeped in Jack Daniel's. I couldn't get Miss Mary's recipe so decided to create my own version.

If you like apples and Bourbon, you're going to love these.

6 Granny Smiths apples

50 g brown sugar

25 g butter

50 ml Bourbon whiskey

Put the butter and sugar into a frying pan and cook until it turns to a dark golden caramel. Core the apples and cut each one into eight wedges and add to the pan. Stir until coated in the caramel. Add the Bourbon, bring back to the boil, remove from the heat, pour into a dish and put into the barbecue (or oven) until the apples are soft and starting to caramelise. Serve with pulled pork – they're also great with ice cream, or on their own!

Cheese Pennies

These great little thin biscuits make ideal nibbles to go with drinks!

125 g sharp Cheddar cheese – grated

125 g Parmesan cheese – grated

100 g salted butter

150 g flour

¼ teaspoon salt

½ teaspoon dry mustard

⅛ teaspoon cayenne pepper

In a medium-sized mixing bowl or food processor, combine all of the ingredients to make a cohesive dough. As soon as the dough starts to come together, gather it into a rough ball. Transfer it to a lightly floured work surface and roll it into a log about 3 cm inches in diameter.

Wrap the log in waxed paper or cling film and chill it in the freezer for 30 minutes. (If you want to freeze them for a longer amount of time, just make sure to remove them from the freezer about 30 minutes before you want to slice them.) Using a serrated knife, slice the log crosswise into 2 mm thick rounds. Place them on a parchment-lined baking sheet. (They won't spread much as they bake.)

Bake the cheese pennies in a preheated oven at 200°C for 12 to 14 minutes, or until they're just beginning to brown. Remove them from the oven and allow them to cool on the pan for several minutes before transferring them to racks to cool completely.

Pulled Pork Egg

I came up with this recipe in the middle of the night and after a quick trial in the morning. It became a hit on my restaurant menu.

100 g potatoes *(Maris Piper or King Edward)*

250 g pulled pork – coarsely chopped

1 teaspoon salt

1 teaspoon pepper

1 teaspoon smoked paprika

Panko breadcrumbs to coat

Boil, drain and mash the potatoes, allow to cool completely. Mix the chopped pulled pork with the potatoes until completely combined, add the seasonings and taste – add more seasoning if needed. Divide the mixture into two equal portions, flatten out, place the egg in the middle and bring the mixture around the egg in a ball to cover it evenly. Coat with panko breadcrumbs, gently pressing them into the egg.

Smoke at 110°C for 1 hour and serve.

A Hatching of Scotch Eggs

Six variations to the simple Scotch Egg – each recipe covers two eggs.

First, boil the eggs: place two eggs in a small saucepan, cover with cold water and put on the heat. Bring to the boil and cook for four minutes. Drain and place under running cold water to cool the eggs quickly. Peel the eggs and leave to get cold. Dust eggs with seasoned flour.

The Breakfast Egg

Breakfast in one little bundle.

300 g pork sausage meat	Pinch of salt and pepper
2 eggs	4 rashers of streaky bacon
100 g black pudding	

In a bowl, break up the black pudding and mix with the sausage meat, salt and pepper, mix well. Divide the mixture into two equal portions, flatten out, place the egg in the middle and bring the mixture around the egg in a ball to cover it evenly. Wrap each egg with two rashers of streaky bacon, ensuring all the bacon ends finish at the bottom. Smoke at 110°C for 1 hour 30 minutes. Rest for 10 minutes, then serve.

The Festive Egg

Some of your favourite festive flavours.

300 g pork sausage meat	4 rashers of streaky bacon
80 g chestnuts	Pinch of salt and pepper
40 g dried cranberries	

Roughly chop the chestnuts and mix with the sausage meat, dried cranberries, salt and pepper. Divide the mixture into two equal portions, flatten out, place the egg in the middle and bring the mixture around the egg in a ball to cover it evenly. Wrap two rashers of bacon around each ball, ensuring all the ends of the bacon are at the bottom. Smoke at 110°C for one hour 30 minutes. Rest for 10 minutes, then serve.

The Fruity Egg

Delicately fruity yet satisfying.

300 g pork sausage meat	1 tablespoon chives – chopped
100 g Bramley apple	Pinch of salt and pepper
Zest and juice of ½ lemon	20 g pork scratchings and 50 g panko breadcrumbs to coat

Grate the apple into a bowl and add lemon zest and juice. Mix with the sausage meat, chives, salt and pepper. Divide the mixture into two equal portions, flatten out, place the egg in the middle and bring the mixture around the egg in a ball to cover it evenly. Blend the pork scratchings to form a crumb and mix with the panko breadcrumbs. Coat with the scratchings and breadcrumb mix, gently pressing the mix into the meat.

Smoke at 110°C for 1 hour 30 minutes. Rest for 10 minutes, then serve.

The Thai Style Egg

Bursting with Thai flavours.

300 g pork sausage meat	1 tablespoon coconut cream
5 g lemon grass	½ teaspoon fish sauce
5 g fresh red chilli	10 g fresh coriander
1 kaffir lime leaf	5 g fresh basil
1 clove of garlic	5 g fresh mint
1 teaspoon oil	Panko breadcrumbs to coat.

Finely chop the lemon grass, red chilli, kaffir lime leaf and garlic. Place in a small pan with the oil and fry for a few minutes until softened, leave to cool. Finely chop the herbs. Mix all the ingredients with the sausage meat until fully combined, divide the mixture into two equal portions, flatten out, place the egg in the middle and bring the mixture around the egg in a ball to cover it evenly. Coat with panko breadcrumbs, gently pressing them into the egg.

Smoke at 110°C for one hour 30 minutes. Rest for 10 minutes, then serve.

The Herby Egg

Fresh, savoury and tasty.

300 g pork sausage meat	1 tablespoon fresh parsley
1 tablespoon fresh sage	Pinch of salt and pepper
1 tablespoon fresh chives	Panko breadcrumbs to coat.

Finely chop the herbs and mix with the sausage meat, salt and pepper. Divide the mixture into two equal portions, flatten out, place the egg in the middle and bring the mixture around the egg in a ball to cover it evenly. Coat with panko breadcrumbs, gently pressing them into the egg.

Smoke at 110°C for 1 hour 30 minutes. Rest for 10 minutes, then serve.

The Chinese Siu Mai Style Egg

The addition of raw prawns makes an interesting twist.

300 g pork sausage meat

75 g raw prawns – finely chopped

2 cm piece of fresh ginger – grated

1 clove of garlic – grated

½ teaspoon five-spice powder

Pinch of salt and pepper

Panko breadcrumbs to coat

Grate garlic and ginger into a bowl. Add the finely chopped raw prawns, sausage meat, five-spice powder, salt and pepper: mix well. Divide the mixture into two equal portions, flatten out, place the egg in the middle and bring the mixture around the egg in a ball to cover it evenly. Coat with panko breadcrumbs, gently pressing them into the egg.

Smoke at 110°C for 1 hour 30 minutes. Rest for 10 minutes, then serve.

'Armadillo' Eggs

These are really tasty things to take on a picnic or packed lunch

250 g pork sausage meat

250 g minced beef

100 g crustless white bread – cubed

50 ml milk

Herbs and spices of your choice

Salt and pepper

Filling

5 jalapenos or baby sweet peppers

Small tub of full fat soft cheese

100 g Cheddar – grated

100 g Red Leicester – grated

1 or 2 bird's eye chillies – finely chopped

Streaky bacon

Cut the top stalk section off the chilli or sweet pepper – scrape the membrane and seeds out of the chilli or pepper with the handle of a teaspoon. Mix the soft cheese with the grated cheeses and chilli and fill the chilli or pepper with this mix, set aside.

Mash together the bread and milk, add your choice of herbs and spices and then mix in the mince and sausage meat, continue mixing until everything is evenly distributed.

Take some of the meat mixture and flatten it in your hand, place the filled chilli or pepper in the centre and wrap the meat around evenly until the filling is total sealed in and you have a rugby shaped ball. Wrap each ball with 1 rasher of 'stretched' streaky bacon.

Place in the smoker at 140°C for around 1-2 hours until cooked.

Mac 'n' Cheese Balls

Gooey, crisp tasty little mouthfuls of mac 'n' cheesy love! These can be made with leftover mac 'n' cheese, or made from scratch with this recipe.

400 g cooked macaroni – chopped

300 ml milk

100 g Cheddar cheese – grated

50 g butter

50 g plain flour

50 g mozzarella cheese – grated

25 g Parmesan cheese – grated

1 tablespoon chives – chopped

1 teaspoon smoked paprika

1 teaspoon red chilli flakes

Salt and pepper

Make a roux from the butter and plain flour and cook for approximately five minutes. Add red pepper flakes (or chilli powder) and chives... mix well. Whisk in the milk and cook gently until quite thick. Leave to cool. Season well with salt and pepper, add smoked paprika and grated cheeses and mix well. Roughly chop the pasta and mix into sauce until incorporated.

Form mix into small balls (about 2 cm diameter). Toss in seasoned flour, then in beaten egg and then into breadcrumbs. Leave to set in the fridge. Deep fry at 180°C until golden brown and serve immediately.

Cheesy Moinks

A play on the combination of moo and oink, moinks are a great barbecue canapé to keep your friends happy while waiting for the main barbecue foods!

250 g minced beef

250 g sausage meat

4 slices of white bread – crusts removed

50 ml milk

100 g hard cheese – cut into cubes

2½ tablespoons beef rub or seasoning

Streaky bacon

Tear the bread into pieces, add the milk and beef rub and mash together by hand. Mix the meats and the bread mix together until fully distributed. Add other herbs and spices of your choice at this stage if you wish.

Take a ball of the meaty mix (approximately golf ball size), flatten on your hand, place a cube of cheese in the centre and form the meat around the cheese before rolling into a ball. Make sure the cheese is sealed inside the meat or it will leak out during cooking, leaving an empty ball and disappointment from the person eating it. Repeat until all the meat is used.

Wrap each ball with a half a stretched rasher of streaky bacon. Cook over indirect heat for 1–2 hours at 140°C, or until a food probe registers above 75°C. Serve as a barbecue canapé or starter. These are also wonderful warmed in a tomato and onion ragu served on spaghetti.

Cheese, Onion and Jalapeno Hush Puppies

Tasty little savoury doughnut balls. You can vary the flavour by using different cheeses: try Stilton and crispy bacon!

150 g polenta or cornmeal	½ teaspoon ground black pepper
75 g self-raising flour	60 g Cheddar cheese – finely grated
1 tablespoon caster sugar	50 g pickled jalapenos – chopped
1 teaspoon baking powder	25 g onion – grated
½ teaspoon cayenne pepper	250 ml buttermilk
½ teaspoon salt	1 egg

Mix all dry ingredients together; add the cheese, jalapenos and onion. Whisk buttermilk and egg together and add to the dry mix to form a thick batter. Leave to rest for at least 10 minutes. Heat fryer to 180°C. Using an oiled round spoon (or small ice cream scoop), drop small balls of the batter into the fryer and cook for 3–4 minutes until puffed up and golden brown. Do not overcrowd the fryer.

When cooked, drain on kitchen paper and serve immediately.

Simple Bourbon Pit Beans

You could make barbecue beans from scratch but sometimes life is just too short to mess around. This is my go to recipe for pit beans: it's quick and easy, and everyone seems to love them.

4 x 440 g cans of baked beans in tomato sauce	4 tablespoons maple syrup
2 large onions – diced	4 tablespoons barbecue sauce
500 g leftover brisket or pulled pork *(optional)*	150 ml Bourbon whiskey
250 g streaky bacon – chopped	2 tablespoons Worcestershire sauce
2 tablespoons barbecue rub	Salt and pepper to taste

Fry the bacon until crisp, add the diced onion and cook until softened and lightly browned. Add the barbecue rub and continue to cook for a couple of minutes. Add the barbecue sauce, maple syrup, Bourbon and the chopped brisket or pulled pork, if using, cook for 15 minutes. Add the remaining ingredients and simmer for an hour or so until thickened.

Loaded Cornbread

If using bacon, cut into strips and fry until crisp. Dice the onion and fry until fully cooked and slightly caramelised. Add the butter and heat until melted. Remove from the heat and add the frozen sweetcorn to help cool the mixture. Preheat oven or barbecue to 175°C...

Grease a baking pan with butter. Mix together the cornmeal, flour, bicarbonate of soda and salt, in a large bowl. Add the buttermilk and eggs to the dry ingredients, mix until just combined... do not over-mix. Add the cooled onion, bacon, butter, sweetcorn mix along with the jalapenos and cheddar, mix lightly to combine.

Pour the mixture into the greased pan and bake for 30-40 minutes until golden brown and a skewer comes out clean when inserted into the centre.

When cooked, remove from oven, allow to sit in pan for 5 minutes before cutting into squares. It's best eaten warm.

If you have any leftover corn bread, try it sliced and fried in butter.

A Southern Staple, cornbread is a great side dish to serve with barbecue. This is my take on what I feel can be a fairly bland side dish. It's been very popular on our barbecue classes.

115 g melted butter
(plus extra butter for greasing baking pan)

300 g buttermilk

2 eggs

150 g cornmeal or polenta

130 g plain flour

1 teaspoon bicarbonate of soda

½ teaspoon salt

100 g frozen sweetcorn kernels

50 g pickled or fresh jalapenos – chopped

150 g grated cheddar

1 onion, finely diced

200 g streaky bacon *(optional)*

Bacon, Corn, Cheddar and Jalapeno Bread 'Pudding'

Somewhere between a savoury bread pudding and a big chunky omelette, it's a hearty meal in itself, or can be served as a side.

350 g white bread crusts removed (stale is good), cut into 2 cm cubes

20 g butter for greasing a dish

1 tablespoon olive oil

12 rashers streaky smoked bacon *(about 250 g)*

1 large onion – roughly chopped

1 red pepper – chopped

100 g sweetcorn

12 eggs

300 ml double cream

300 ml sour cream

80 g pickled, sliced jalapenos – roughly chopped

250 g strong cheddar cheese – grated

1 teaspoon salt

½ teaspoon black pepper

Heat the oil in a large frying pan and cook the bacon over medium heat until golden brown but not crisp. Transfer the bacon to a plate, cut into pieces and set aside. Add the onion and pepper to the pan and cook over medium heat until softened and lightly browned. Set aside to cool. Whisk the eggs in a large bowl, then whisk in the cream, sour cream, salt and pepper to combine. Add all the ingredients to the bowl with the egg and cream mixture and mix well. The bread should soak up most of the liquid: don't be afraid to use your hand to squeeze the mixture into the bread.

Grease the baking dish with the butter and pour the mix into the dish. If making in advance, wrap the dish tightly in cling film and refrigerate for up to 24 hours. Bake at around 160°C in the barbecue, until golden-brown and puffy and the edges have pulled away slightly from the sides of the dish (45 to 50 minutes).

Serve straight from the dish.

||||||||||||||||||||||||||||||||||||||||||||||||||||||||

Sublime Smoked Nuts

These wonderfully smoky nuts can be eaten on their own or chopped and used in a salad.

500 g mixed nuts *(cashews, walnuts, almonds, hazelnuts, pecans and Brazil nuts all work really well)*

20 ml butter

25 g barbecue rub of your choice

In a large pan, melt the butter. Pour the butter over the nuts and toss until they are coated. Sprinkle the rub over the nuts and toss again so that the rub sticks to the nuts. Place coated nuts into a large shallow heatproof tray and put into your smoker on a low heat (around 80°C) for 1-2 hours.

FROM THE RIVER TO THE SEA

Sardines and Prawns with Chermoula Sauce

The chermoula is great as a baste and as a dressing with grilled sardines or prawns.

Fresh or frozen whole sardines and king prawns in the shell

Chermoula marinade/ dressing
75 g fresh coriander
30 g fresh parsley
2 cloves garlic

1 preserved lemon *(skin only)*
1 teaspoon ground cumin
½ teaspoon smoked paprika
1 fresh Birdseye Chilli
75 ml olive oil

Either blitz all the marinade/dressing ingredients together in a blender or finely chop everything and mix together in a bowl.

Thread sardines (lightly slash the skins) and prawns onto skewers. If using wooden skewers, soak them first.

Place half of the sauce into a bowl and use a brush to baste the fish/prawns. Barbecue over direct heat until the skin of the sardines is blistered and the fish is cooked.

Serve the fish with the remaining sauce.

Smoke-Kissed Prawns with a Grilled Salad

Who can resist these prawns, touched by a smoky kiss, served with a warm, grilled salad?

1 kg raw tiger prawns *(fresh or defrosted)*
3 cloves garlic – minced
½ red chilli – finely chopped
80 ml light olive oil
60 ml tomato ketchup
30 ml red wine vinegar

5 g chopped fresh basil
½ teaspoon sugar
½ teaspoon salt
¼ teaspoon cayenne pepper
Little gem lettuces
Heritage cherry and plum tomatoes

De-vein and peel the prawns, leaving just the tail section on.

In a large bowl, mix together the garlic, olive oil, tomato ketchup, red wine vinegar, chilli, basil, salt and cayenne pepper. Add prawns to the bowl and stir until evenly coated. Cover and refrigerate for 30 minutes to 1 hour, stirring once or twice.

Preheat smoker to 140°C. Lightly oil grill grate. Lay prawns out onto grill rack ensuring that there is a small gap between each one. Add a small piece of mild wood (such as ash or alder) to the smoker.

Cook prawns, on skewers, over indirect heat for approximately 20–30 minutes or until opaque.

Halve the lettuces, drizzle with a little olive oil and place cut side down on the chargrill until coloured. Flip over for another minute and sprinkle with salt.

Place the whole baby tomatoes on the grill and cook until the skin starts to blister and burst. Turn over and repeat on the other side. Drizzle with balsamic glaze and sprinkle with salt.

||||||||||||||||||||||||||||||||||||||||||||||||||||||||

Salmon Belly Bites

I created this lovely dish whilst filleting whole salmon to make smoked salmon. It's the wonderful fatty part of the salmon belly. Cooking it this way is simple and gives a really tasty result. I resisted the temptation to call them Salmon Burnt Ends!

Salmon belly strips
Chicken rub *(see rubs)*

Remove skin from the salmon belly and cut into bite-size squares. Sprinkle with rub and place in a baking pan.

Put into the smoker at around 140°C and cook for approximately 1 hour. Beech wood is lovely with this. Serve hot.

Rum-Soaked Hot Smoked Salmon

The ingredients for this recipe are not set in stone and can be substituted with something similar, say wild sea trout instead of salmon and your own choice of rum or Bourbon whiskey.

Salmon side or fillet – pin-bones removed

150 ml rum of your choice *(Bourbon also works)*

The cure
1 tablespoon dill weed
150 g brown sugar
200 g sea salt

Lay the salmon (skin side up) in a shallow dish, as small as the salmon to save wasting the rum. Pour enough rum to cover. Leave for 30 minutes – do not leave any longer than this, as the salmon will start to cook. Drain the rum.

Sprinkle the dill weed over the meaty side of the salmon, followed by the sugar and salt. Cover and leave to cure in the fridge for 1 to 4 hours. (The longer you leave it the firmer the fish will become, but don't leave for longer than 4 hours.) Remove salmon from the cure and rinse under cold running water. Most of the dill will remain stuck to the salmon: this is good. Pat dry with kitchen towel... This is important, as the fish will take the smoke better when dry.

Place skin side down on the grill of the smoker and cook on a low heat (approx. 110°C) until the fish turns from translucent to opaque and is cooked. (Probe temperature 62°C.) Remove from smoker and serve. Alternatively, cool quickly, cover and refrigerate to serve cold.

To serve, remove skin and either cut into slices or break into large flakes.

Louisiana Devilled Crab Cakes

These wonderful crab patties can be served with a salad or in a bun, burger style!

250 g white crab meat *(fresh or tinned)*

100 g fresh breadcrumbs

3 tablespoons melted butter

1 large egg

1 stick celery – finely chopped

1 spring onion – finely sliced

½ onion – finely chopped

½ green pepper – finely chopped

1 tablespoon sweet chilli sauce

1 tablespoon vegetable oil

1 tablespoon sour cream

¾ teaspoon cayenne pepper

½ teaspoon salt

½ teaspoon mustard powder

½ teaspoon Worcestershire sauce

Fry onion, pepper and celery in one tablespoon of butter over a moderately low heat, stirring occasionally, until vegetables are softened. Set aside to cool.

Whisk together egg, sour cream, mustard, Worcestershire sauce, cayenne and salt in a large bowl, then stir in spring onion, cooked vegetables and breadcrumbs; finally, gently stir in the crab meat.

Form into six cakes (approx. 5 cm in diameter).

Heat oil and remaining two tablespoons butter in frying pan over moderate heat until foam subsides, then cook crab cakes, turning once, until golden brown.

Serve with lemon and lime wedges.

Atlantic Coast Red Snapper

Red snapper is quite a strong fish but holds its own against the chimichurri dressing.

Red snapper fillets

Olive oil

Salt and pepper to season

Lime wedge

Chimichurri dressing

100 ml cider vinegar

1 teaspoon salt

2 garlic cloves

1 red chilli

Small bunch fresh coriander

Small bunch fresh parsley

100 ml olive oil

Cut the snapper side into 90 g fillets and pat them dry with kitchen towel to remove any excess moisture. Season and oil the fish and place the fillets skin side down, onto a hot barbecue over direct heat.

Cook the fish for a minute until you can see the skin side of the fish starting to sear. Move to a cooler part of the barbecue over indirect heat until the fish is just cooked. Turn the fish over carefully for a second just to seal the other side.

To serve, stack the fillets on top of each other neatly on a plate and dress with the chimichurri. Garnish with lime and baby leaves.

For the chimichurri dressing: finely chop the coriander and parsley. De-seed and finely dice the chilli, crush or grate the garlic...mix everything together.

If you're not great at chopping, put the garlic and chilli into a blender and blend until finely chopped. Add the herbs and pulse until chopped then add the other ingredients and pulse a few more times until incorporated.

CHICKEN AND FEATHERED GAME

Beer Can Chicken

Some people think that sitting a chicken over a can of beer does nothing. I don't agree. I think it adds moisture and flavour, but most of all, it looks pretty good and makes people smile!

100 ml beer or cider
Olive oil for rubbing

1 whole chicken
(weighing around 2–3 kg)
Chicken rub

Whilst some people use the can itself to sit the chicken on, I do tend to ask myself whether the printing on the can could release toxins when heated, so I prefer to use a special beer can chicken holder. There are loads out there on the market, so just grab yourself one and stay safe.

Pour the beer or cider into your chicken holder, rub chicken with oil and sprinkle with chicken rub inside and out - slide the chicken over the chicken holder (drumsticks pointing downwards) so that the bird sits upright. Use a small potato or a crumpled-up piece of foil to block the neck hole of the chicken to stop the steam escaping.

Place the chicken with the beer can upright in roasting tray into your smoker. The temperature should sit at around 130–140°C. Add some hickory or Bourbon barrel wood to the fire to create the smoke. Cooking takes approximately 2½ to 3 hours, but we suggest you use a meat probe to ensure correct temperature (over 75°C). Ensure the juices run clear before you remove from the barbecue.

Take care when removing the chicken from the holder as there will be hot liquid in the beer holder.

Remember, smoked chicken will have a pink tint to the surface of the meat. This is known as a smoke ring and is perfectly normal. *(Not to be confused with a pink rawness next to the bone, which means you need to cook it for longer.)*

||||||||||||||||||||||||||||||||||||||||||||||||||||||||

Spatchcock Chicken

1 whole chicken
Olive oil

Rub of your choice

Lay the chicken breast down and use poultry shears to cut down either side of the backbone, as close to the bone as possible.

Turn the chicken over (breast side up) and pull out the sides, then push down on the breastbone: you should hear a crack as the wishbone breaks.

Rub both sides of the chicken with olive oil and sprinkle with a rub of your choice.

Barbecue indirect, breast side up, at around 140°C for approximately 2–3 hours or until cooked (probes above 75°C).

Alabama Fried Chicken 'Burger'

This uses a 'Southern Fried' Style Chicken Escalope as the burger.

4 chicken breasts	1 tablespoon lemon pepper
200 ml buttermilk	
100 g flour	1 teaspoon salt
50 g cornflour	½ teaspoon cayenne
50 g cornmeal	

Butterfly each chicken breast, sandwich between two pieces of cling film and bash them out to an even thickness. Place the buttermilk into a bowl and add the chicken. Cover and refrigerate for up to 12 hours.

When ready to cook, mix all of the dry ingredients together and coat the buttermilk chicken in them, ensuring the whole escalope is well covered. Shake off any excess and deep fry at 170°C for approximately 5–7 minutes. Serve in a brioche-style bun with cheese, mayonnaise, lettuce and tomato.

Chicken Doner Style Kebab

This dish always goes down well on our barbecue classes. It's also a great dish to get your children involved in preparing food.

2 kg chicken thighs – skin and bone removed	100 g chicken rub or a spice paste of your choice
500 g Greek Style yoghurt *(full fat is better)*	

Make a marinade by mixing the yoghurt with the chicken rub (you can use any spice mix for this).

Marinate the chicken for a couple of hours or overnight. The yoghurt will help to tenderise the chicken.

Thread the chicken onto a large upright skewer or rotisserie, turning each piece a ¼ turn so that you end up with a rounded skewer of chicken.

Cook over indirect heat at 140°C until the chicken is cooked (probes above 75°C). This will take around 3 hours.

To serve, slice down the chicken thighs and serve on flatbreads or in pitta bread with salad.

Barbecue Buffalo Style Chicken Wings

1 kg chicken wings

75 g chicken rub

2 tablespoons cornflour

Remove and discard the wing tip, then cut the wing into two pieces, the drumette and the flat (see picture below).

In a large bowl or bag, mix together all of the dry ingredients thoroughly. Add the chicken wing pieces and toss until they are evenly coated, shake off excess flour and lay out in a single layer on a tray. Refrigerate for around an hour if you can.

Cook over indirect heat on a barbecue set to around 150°C until probe hits above 75°C (approximately 30 minutes). You can also cook at a lower temperature for a longer period if you prefer. Add a small piece of wood if you want a smokier flavour.

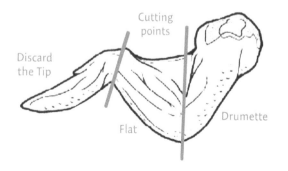

Making the Sauce

Do this a few days in advance if possible to allow the vinegar to mellow.

250 g American Mustard

150 g caster sugar

100 g cider vinegar

5 g ground black pepper

3 g sea salt

30 g butter

200 ml Frank's RedHot sauce

Place all the ingredients into a pan, **except the butter and Frank's sauce**... Bring to the boil. Once boiling, remove from the heat and add the butter. Whisk to make a smooth emulsion. Add as much of the Frank's RedHot sauce as you wish (probably half a bottle to start with). Place wings in a lidded container, pour over enough sauce to coat the wings and then toss them in the sauce until coated.

Serve with sticks of carrot and celery and some blue cheese dip.

Chicken Cobbler

I love making this with leftover smoked chicken; it's simple and quick to make. The recipe also works really well with leftover smoked turkey.

250 g cooked smoked chicken – shredded or cubed

50 g smoked streaky bacon

1 onion – finely diced

75 g plain flour

75 g butter

150 ml chicken stock

150 ml milk

100 g frozen peas

100 g frozen sweetcorn

Cobbler Topping

250 g plain flour

2½ teaspoons baking powder

½ teaspoon salt

75 g butter

180 ml milk

To make the cobbler topping, place the flour, baking powder and salt in a bowl. Rub in the cold butter until it resembles breadcrumbs and add the milk gradually until you make a soft, damp dough. Wrap in cling film and leave in the fridge to rest.

In a frying pan, fry the onion until translucent, add the bacon and cook until the fat has rendered.

Add the butter and flour, cook out for two minutes before adding the chicken stock and milk. Cook until thickened and remove from the heat.

Add the peas and sweetcorn, then gently mix in the chicken, before placing in a shallow ovenproof dish.

Roll out the rested dough to around a 2 cm thickness, cut into rounds, or whatever shape you fancy. Set each disk of dough on top of the filling, leaving spaces in between each disk.

Place in a pre-heated barbecue or oven at 180°C for around 30 minutes, until the cobbler is golden brown.

Serve.

Brined Smoked Turkey

I've used this recipe for years and it has never let me down. It produces a delicately smoked, moist and tender bird. The smoke flavour develops more when the bird is cold and it makes great sandwiches!

1 fresh turkey, or turkey crown

The brine
4 litres cold water
125 g salt
100 g caster sugar
100 g brown sugar
150 ml light soy sauce
100 ml cider vinegar
50 g runny honey
3 tablespoons ground black pepper

1 tablespoon garlic granules
1 teaspoon ground allspice
1 orange and 1 lemon – sliced

The baste
150 g butter – chilled and rolled flat
1 orange and 1 lemon – quartered

Mix the brine ingredients in a large food-grade plastic bucket, bag or other non-metallic container, until sugars and salt are dissolved. Put the turkey in the brine and cover (ensure it is submerged). Place in fridge overnight, or for up to – but no longer than – 24 hours.

Before cooking, drain the turkey and leave to dry a little (or pat dry with paper towels). Insert a quartered apple and orange into the cavity of the bird. Set the barbecue to 140 –150°C (indirect heat).

Loosen the skin on the turkey breast, being careful not to tear it, and work some cold flattened pieces of butter between the skin and the meat.

Cook the turkey until the internal temperature measures above 72°C: you should allow a cooking time of approximately 1 hour per kilo.

Always plan to start cooking your turkey a couple of hours earlier than you think it will be done. This will allow for any temperature variations and also give you lots of time to rest the bird before carving.

Probe the meat away from the bone in the thickest part of the thigh (or breast if you're cooking a turkey crown) to ensure that the internal temperature measures above 72°C. Continue to cook until it does.

Transfer to a warm place and leave to rest (covered) until ready to serve. Rest for at least 30 minutes before carving.

Smoked Duck and Mango Salad

This is a lovely summer salad. I'm not usually a fan of fruit in savoury dishes. However, mango goes so well with smoked duck that I became a convert!

2 duck breasts

1 tablespoon sea salt

Salad

Mixed salad leaves

1 fresh mango, cut into small cubes

Smoked sourdough bread croutons

Strawberry balsamic dressing *(see below)*

Baby plum or cherry tomatoes, halved

Score the skin of the duck breast, taking care not to cut into the flesh. Sprinkle the skin with some sea salt. Leave for at least 30 minutes before placing in a smoker at around 100°C. Leave to smoke for around 2 hours. Maple is a really good wood to use for this.

Remove the duck from the smoker and place skin side down in a frying pan. Turn on the heat and cook over a medium heat until the skin renders and crisps up. Remove from the pan and chill.

In a bowl, mix together the salad leaves with some strawberry balsamic dressing, toss until coated. To make the smoked bread croutons, cube some stale bread (sourdough works well), toss in olive oil, salt and pepper, then place in smoker until crisp.

Place the dressed salad leaves in a serving dish and add the halved baby plum or cherry tomatoes, the cubed mango and croutons.

Slice the **cold** duck breast into thin slices (approx. 2 mm thick) across the grain.

Neatly lay the whole sliced duck breasts on top of the salad. Drizzle a little more strawberry balsamic dressing over the top and serve.

TIP: *Save the rendered fat for roasting potatoes another day.*

Strawberry Balsamic Dressing

250 ml balsamic vinegar

100 g strawberry jam

125 ml olive oil

Place balsamic vinegar and jam into a pan, bring to the boil and reduce until only approximately half remains. Leave to cool.

Add the oil and, using a stick blender, blend the mixture to form an emulsion. Decant into a squeeze bottle and use within six months.

Grilled Lemon Yogurt Chicken

Bursting with flavour and lower in calories, this is a great dish for those long summer days!

4 chicken breasts, butterflied

200 ml buttermilk

1 lemon, zest and juice

1 tablespoon olive oil

4 cloves garlic, crushed

1 teaspoon smoked paprika

1 teaspoon salt

1 teaspoon lemon pepper

Dressing

50 g natural Greek style yoghurt

1 tablespoon harissa paste

Butterfly each chicken breast, place between two sheets of cling film and pound them out to an even thickness. Whisk together the buttermilk, the lemon zest and juice, olive oil, garlic, smoked paprika, salt and lemon pepper in a dish, add chicken, coat with the marinade, leave in refrigerator for at least 3 hours. Remove chicken from the dish and place directly onto a preheated barbecue grill (indirect heat) cook on both sides until well browned and no longer pink in the centre, 10–20 minutes. For the dressing, combine yogurt and harissa in a small bowl. Serve chicken, sliced on top of a crisp green salad with the dressing mixture on the side.

MEAT: BEEF

Slow Smoked Mocha Rubbed Beef Short Ribs

Beef Short ribs are a popular cut of beef. They are cut from the rib and plate, plus a small corner of the square-cut chuck. The Mocha rub gives them a lovely rich flavour.

Beef short ribs *(I prefer the three or four bone sections, also known as Jacob's ladders)*

Dark beer or cherry juice

Mocha Rub

2 tablespoons fine sea salt

2 tablespoons coarse ground black pepper

2 tablespoons unsweetened cocoa powder

2 tablespoons ground coffee *(not instant coffee)*

1 tablespoon light brown sugar

1 teaspoon ground coriander

1 teaspoon ground cinnamon

1 teaspoon ground chilli powder

1 teaspoon smoked paprika

8 juniper berries – crushed

First make the rub. Put the juniper berries in a grinder or a pestle and mortar with some salt and grind. Mix all the other rub ingredients with the juniper mix until well combined.

Trim any excess fat from the beef short ribs and score both the membrane and the fat sides of the ribs in a criss-cross pattern.

Sprinkle the rub over the meaty side of the short rib. Leave to sit for at least one hour to allow the spices to permeate the meat. In the meantime, prepare your barbecue using the minion method with a chunk of cherry wood or some pre-soaked Bourbon wood chips. Get it to a constant temperature of 140°C

Place the meat into the barbecue, bone side down, and close the lid.

Cook for 2–3 hours until a nice crust has formed. Remove from the barbecue place in a baking pan, bone side down. Add some dark beer or cherry juice and cover with foil. Return

to the barbecue for another 3–4 hours until the meat is really soft and tender. It should be almost falling off the bone: if it isn't, continue to cook until it is.

Allow to rest for 30 minutes in the foil before serving.

Reverse Seared Tomahawk Steak with Smoked Bone Marrow Potato Mash

I received this baby as a Christmas present from my butcher. I took one look at it and knew this was the only way to do it justice – it was amazing!

1 aged tomahawk steak	Mash
Sea salt flakes	Canoe-cut beef bones
Cracked black pepper	Maris Piper potatoes
1 clove of garlic	Butter

First season your steak, rub with the clove of garlic and then sprinkle with salt and pepper. Setup your smoker as low a temperature as you can get (aim for 100°C), indirect heat. Put the seasoned, well chilled, tomahawk and the canoe cut bones onto the smoker and leave to gently smoke for around 1-2 hours. The aim is for the steak to take smoke and cook to an internal temperature of around 52°C.

Whilst the steak is smoking, peel the potatoes and boil in salted water. When cooked, drain and mash with as much butter as you wish and season to taste. When the bones are smoked, scrape out the marrow and mash it into the potatoes, piping the potato into the bones as a nice way of serving.

Remove from the smoker and crank up the heat for the sear. You want to get to around 250°C, direct heat.

Put the steak onto the grill and sear on both sides until you achieve an internal temperature of 56°C for medium rare. Rest for at least 15 minutes before serving.

Maltese Beef Olives (Bragoli) with a Kiss of Smoke

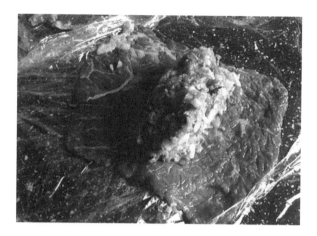

A little diversion back to my heritage. My parents were both Maltese and moved to England in the 1950s. This is one of my late mum's recipes that I grew up with. I've tweaked it a little to include some smoke. In Malta, they're called Bragoli. The sauce can be served with pasta as a first course, leaving the Bragoli to be served as the main course with mashed potatoes and vegetables. Mum also used to make this as one huge Bragoli by making a pocket in a whole of skirt of beef, stuffing the mixture into it and sewing it up again!

4 thin slices of rump steak

Stuffing
250 g lean minced beef
75 g finely diced bacon
1 onion – finely chopped
1 egg – hard boiled
1 egg – raw
1 tablespoon chopped parsley
1 carrot – grated
2 bacon rashers – chopped
Salt and pepper

Sauce
2 large onions – chopped
3 cloves garlic – crushed
1 tin of tomatoes (400 g)
1 teaspoon tomato paste
2 carrots – diced
150 g frozen peas
2 medium size potatoes – peeled and diced
2 bay leaves
100 ml red wine
1 teaspoon sugar
1 beef stock cube
Freshly ground pepper

Combine all the stuffing ingredients in a bowl. Place the meat slices on a chopping board, cover with cling film and flatten with a kitchen mallet. Spoon the stuffing onto the centre of each slice and roll it up. Tightly wrap in cling film and refrigerate for a couple of hours to set the shape.

Place the beef olives in the smoker over indirect heat at 110°C and smoke for approximately 2 hours.

Cook the onions and garlic for a few minutes in a large pan, add the carrots, potatoes, tomatoes and fry for another 5 minutes. Add the tomato paste, sugar, stock cube, bay leaves and wine to the pan and stir. Season with pepper and cook for about 15 minutes.

Put the smoked beef olives back into the saucepan and add the peas. Bring to the boil and return to the smoker for an hour or until the meat is tender and the sauce has reduced and thickened.

Serve on a bed of linguine or with mashed potatoes.

Sloppy Joes

This rich, thick concoction is perfect served in a hamburger bun, or try serving it on a classic hot dog and topped with cheese. Whichever you choose, don't expect clean faces or hands afterwards!

500 g minced beef

70 g tomato purée

250 ml beef stock

1 large onion – finely chopped

2 cloves garlic – finely chopped

1 red chilli – finely chopped

1 tablespoon sugar

1 tablespoon American mustard

1 teaspoon chilli powder *(more if you like it hot)*

1 teaspoon Worcestershire sauce

1 teaspoon salt

1 teaspoon celery seeds

½ teaspoon ground cumin

½ teaspoon fresh ground black pepper

Fry the onion until softened, add the minced beef and continue to fry. When the meat is nearly done, add the garlic. Add the remaining ingredients and stir well to combine.

Simmer over a low heat, uncovered, until the meat is tender and the sauce has thickened (approx. 1 hour).

Serve either in a hamburger bun or on top of hot dogs in rolls topped with cheese, jalapenos or whatever takes your fancy.

Texas Brisket Chilli

You can't beat a good chilli, and I think this is a pretty good chilli. It's a great way to use up any leftover smoked brisket...add more chillies if you want it hotter!

500 g smoked beef brisket

1 tablespoon olive oil

2 medium onions, ½ cm diced

2 garlic cloves, chopped

2 red peppers, ½ cm diced

2 green peppers, ½ cm diced

2 jalapeno chillies – finely diced

2 Birdseye chillies – finely chopped

2 teaspoons ground coriander

2 teaspoons chilli powder

2 tablespoons tomato purée

2 teaspoons ground cumin

1 teaspoon smoked paprika

1 tin chopped tomatoes

1 teaspoon caster sugar

100 ml beef stock

1 bay leaf

Salt and pepper to taste

Heat the oil in a large saucepan and cook the onion until lightly browned. Add the garlic, red and green peppers and fry until tender, stirring occasionally. Add the coriander, cumin, paprika and chilli powder and cook for a couple of minutes. Stir in the tomato purée and cook it for a further 5 minutes.

Add chopped brisket, followed by the tomatoes, stock, sugar and bay leaf. Season with salt and pepper. Increase the heat and bring to the boil. Then reduce heat, cover and simmer gently for 1 hour until thickened. (This part can be done on the smoker for an extra smoky flavour.)

Serve with a mixture of brown and white rice, grated cheese, sour cream, pickled jalapenos and tortilla chips.

Bacon Wrapped Meat Bomb

I grew up eating my mum's meatloaf. I wasn't much of a fan of it, to be honest, but after a lot of tweaking I have totally transformed it to this recipe, which I would be happy to eat any time!

250 g beef mince

250 g pork sausage meat

1 tablespoon oil

1 green pepper

1 medium onion

1 jalapeno *(or six slices of pickled Jalapeno)*

2 cloves garlic

100 g fresh breadcrumbs

2 tablespoons Worcestershire sauce

1 teaspoon salt

1 teaspoon black pepper

8 rashers of streaky bacon

80 g block of cheese *(optional)*

Finely chop the green pepper, onion, garlic and jalapeno pepper and fry until tender. Leave to cool.

Place all ingredients into a large bowl and mix well.

Make a bacon lattice by weaving rashers of bacon in and out until you have a flat slab of woven bacon – you can do this on a piece of cling film to make it easier to roll, but make sure you remove it all at the end.

Pack half of the meat mixture onto one end of the lattice and push the cheese block along the centre before topping with the remaining meat. Make sure you seal the meat together ,or the cheese with leak out. Roll the lattice tightly: it should overlap slightly at the end.

Place into smoker with the seam of the bacon at the bottom and cook at 125°C for around 3 hours, or until the internal temperature reaches above 75°C.

||||||||||||||||||||||||||||||||||||||||||||||||||||||||||||

Low 'n' Slow Smoked Pichana

Pichana, also known as tri-tip and top rump, is a cut of meat that is becoming more and more popular in the UK. It's a tasty and tender cut when handled correctly.

1 whole pichana

1 teaspoon salt

1 teaspoon pepper

1 teaspoon garlic granules

1 teaspoon finely chopped fresh rosemary

Mix the salt, pepper, garlic granules and rosemary together in a bowl.

Sprinkle it all over the pichana and pat it in gently.

Setup your barbecue – with added cherry wood – to around 100°C indirect heat. Place the meat, fat side down, onto the barbecue grill and leave to cook for around 2–3 hours, or until it probes to an internal temperature of 54°C.

The cooler temperature should cook the meat through but keep it medium rare.

Finish over a high temperature – direct heat – to form a nice finishing crust.

Pichana 'Gaucho Style'

Pichana is also great cut into steaks. This recipe cooks it 'Gaucho' style on a rotisserie.

1 whole pichana

Marinade
4 tablespoons sherry vinegar
4 tablespoons olive oil
2 tablespoons soy sauce

1 tablespoon Worcestershire sauce
1 tablespoon soft brown sugar
1 teaspoon Sriracha sauce
2 cloves garlic – crushed

Mix the marinade in a Ziplock bag.

Cut the Pichana into 4 cm thick steaks (across the narrower side) and add to the marinade bag, seal and leave in the fridge overnight, or as long as possible.

When ready to cook, bend the steaks into a C-shape (fat outwards) and push onto a rotisserie skewer. Cook directly above hot coals (when using my ProQ, I like to leave one of the collars between the fire and the rotisserie ring). Cook until done to your liking: medium rare is best.

Serve sliced straight off the skewer.

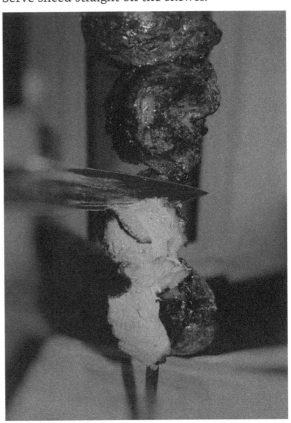

Competition Brisket

It was a tough decision whether to put this in the book or not as it is very much in note form, but this recipe went towards my winning The Jack Daniel's Invitational World Barbecue Championships in 2004. It also won me a 2nd place in the Jack Daniel's Champion of Champions – Winners Circle in 2013.

USDA or Australian beef brisket *(Packer Cut)*
Beef stock jelly
Rub of your choice
Sauce of your choice

Buying – In my opinion, bigger is better, but thickness is key! I aim for a 5–7 kg thick brisket if possible. When producing a top quality product, grade and age are everything. For a contest, I like my brisket aged for at least 45 days. Ageing deepens the beef flavour and helps the meat to be naturally more tender. If you are able to buy briskets that are Cryovac'd, then you can age them yourself in the fridge. Make sure you find out the packing date from your supplier to ensure you have a record of the age.

Trimming – I like to cut the fat off until I get to 3–5 mm thickness on the flat end. I trim almost all of the fat off the point end, as there is enough connective tissue and fat within it to keep it moist and you don't want to lose that lovely bark that's going to form. I also trim the sides of the brisket so that it will fit into the presentation box without having to be trimmed after cooking.

Injecting and Seasoning – If you're injecting, you'll want to do it as soon as possible because of how long it takes to cook a brisket. Most cook-offs won't inspect your meat until noon on the day before turn-in. Once inspected, inject with a good homemade beef bone stock and use a bit more stock to rub over the outside of the meat. Apply your choice of rub – do not cake it on, just coat it lightly and rub (pat in) – I like to use two or three different rubs and layer the flavours, but do be careful not to over-use rubs or you will lose the flavour of the meat. Leave chilled for as long as possible.

Slicing the Brisket

Cooking – If cooking pork and brisket together, I like to put the beef above the pork, as the beef will drip a better flavour onto the pork than the other way around. You should cook with the fat side up. I like to cook for 6-8 hours at 180-200°F (82-93°C) to get as much smoke into the meat as I can. Then I'll put the meat into a large foil pan, add some liquid (either more beef stock, beer or cherry juice), cover with foil and then increase the temperature 225-250°F (107-121°C). Usually this stage will take an additional 4-6 hours, depending on the size of the brisket.

Is it done yet? Here is where experience helps. I use my trusty Thermapen to decide when to take the brisket off, not only by temperature but also by the amount of resistance I get when I put the probe into the meat. The reference temperature for this is usually between 195-205°F (90-96°C). However, it's not done until it feels like it's done. The resistance I like to achieve is similar to putting a warm knife into cold butter. (Always probe from the side not the top.)

I aim to have the brisket done 3-4 hours before turn-in, so that I can rest the meat. It is very important to rest the meat before cutting. When the brisket is done, remove the point section and put it back in the smoker (in the foil pan) to continue cooking for a couple more hours: these will be your 'burnt ends'. Wrap the flat tightly in cling film and foil and hold it in a hotbox until ready to work on your turn-in. Save most of the juices from the foil pan and mix with a little barbecue sauce to make a gravy for the brisket slices. The ratio is ¼-cup beef juice to 2-3 tablespoons of sauce.

My brisket competition turn in box:
Jack Daniel's 2013 Winners Circle – 2nd Place

Competition Presentation

Competition brisket is always presented in a 9-inch lidded food box. When presenting, I like to slice the brisket around 3-4 mm thick. I dip each slice into the heated gravy I made earlier and then arrange in the box.

When displaying the burnt ends, I like to cut a large rectangle out of the point to the size of the area of box I wish to fill and then dip it into the gravy before cutting into cubes. Ensure that the cubes are cut right through and place the whole rectangle of cubed burnt ends into the box at the bottom, so that it looks like one piece, this will help to retain the moisture and heat. Finish by brushing a little of the 'gravy' on top.

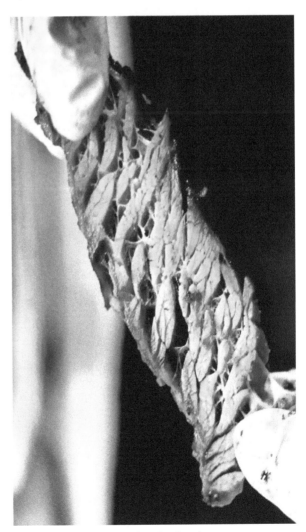

The 'perfect' brisket slice

Beer Can Burgers

- Crispy fried bacon, mushrooms and blue cheese
- Chilli con carne with cheese
- Ham, tomato and cheese
- Mac and cheese
- Leftover barbecue meat with caramelised onion, pickled jalapenos and cheese

The only rule is that if the filling needs to be cooked, cook it first, then fill the burger cup with it and top it with cheese.

Cook over indirect heat at around 150°C for around an hour. The bacon should be nicely browned and the meat cooked through, with the cheesy topping bubbling well. The filling should also be heated through.

You could serve this burger in the traditional way in a bun, but it would be really difficult to eat, so I would suggest serving it with a nice green salad or fries.

These 'monster burgers' make great vessels for all sorts of fillings.

Makes 4

600 g minced beef
1 teaspoon salt

1 teaspoon freshly ground black pepper
12 slices smoked streaky bacon
Filling of your choice *(see below)*

Mix the minced beef with the salt and pepper and separate into 4 x 150 g tightly formed balls.

Cover a beer-sized can with cling film. Press the can into the ball of mince and form it up the sides, around 6 cm high.

Take some streaky bacon and wrap it tightly around the meat until all the sides are covered in bacon, then remove the can. You should be left with cup shapes of beef wrapped in bacon.

Here's where your creativity can go into overdrive. It's time to fill them... here are some suggestions:

My Ultimate Burger Stack

I like to use a mix of chuck steak and short rib for my burgers. I always try to select a cut that has a fair bit of fat as this is what will give you a moist and tasty burger. Try not to handle the meat too much or it will become tough; finally, be careful with fillings, as they are designed to complement the burger, not compete with it.

650 g chuck steak – leave the fat on

350 g short rib

100 g onion – grated

1 tablespoon Dijon mustard

1 tablespoon Worcestershire sauce

2 teaspoons salt

2 teaspoons freshly ground black pepper

Fry the grated onion in olive oil until soft. Set to one side to cool.

Mince the chuck steak and short rib together on a medium plate. Mix the steak with the remaining ingredients, including the cold cooked onion. Do not overwork the mixture.

Divide into equal sized patties (around 170 g each) and shape into burgers. Using your thumb, make a depression in the centre of each patty. This will help to stop the burger puffing up whilst it's cooking. Leave to stand while you heat your barbecue grill or plancha.

Grill your burgers until they are cooked through; you can serve them slightly pink if you prefer. (I like to give them around 3–4 minutes per side.) Turn them only once if possible to prevent the juices running out. Don't prod, squeeze, flatten or poke them, or you'll lose the juices.

Top with the cheese just before the cooking is finished to give it time it to melt.

The Stack

6 brioche buns, sliced horizontally in half and toasted *(see recipe)*

3 red onions – peeled, thinly sliced and fried in a little oil until caramelised

12 rashers of smoked streaky bacon – grilled until almost crisp

6 slices of Monterey Jack Cheese

2 little gem lettuces *(pick the leaves and leave whole)*

6 runny fried eggs

Burger sauce *(see recipe)*

To build the stack, take the bottom half of the brioche bun, spread with some burger sauce and then top with lettuce leaves and some of the caramelised red onion. Place the burger on top, then a slice of tomato followed by two rashers of bacon cheese and a fried egg. Spread the top half of the bun with some more burger sauce then place on top of the rest of the burger.

MEAT: PORK

Hickory Smoked Pork Belly

4 x 250 g pork belly squares – rind removed	Chicken rub
Cider-braised red cabbage	Maple syrup
	Salt

Score the fat of the pork belly, turn over so that the fat side is downwards, brush the meat side of the belly with maple syrup, then sprinkle the rub onto the meat. Turn the meat over again, fat side up, and sprinkle with salt.

Smoke over indirect heat for around 4 hours at 120°C. Transfer fat side down to direct heat to crisp the fat a little, being careful not to burn it.

Serve on a bed of braised red cabbage.

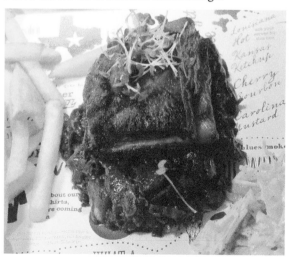

Cider Braised Red Cabbage

1 red cabbage	250 cm vegetable bouillon
4 sticks of celery	1 garlic clove
1 large white onion	2 bay leaves
500 ml apple juice	150 g bramley apple – grated
65 ml cider vinegar	Oil for cooking

Thinly slice the red cabbage, onion, garlic and celery, keeping all ingredients separate for now. Make the vegetable bouillon from a cube or powder.

Heat the oil in a deep pan, add the onions and celery and sweat for 5 minutes until soft. Add the red cabbage and cook for a further 2 minutes. Add all the other ingredients except the apples. Cook the cabbage until tender. Stir in the grated apple, season to taste, heat through and serve.

WAIT! ..IT'S A GREAT IDEA ...

Porchetta

1 x 3 to 4 kg piece of boneless pork loin with the skin on

Filling

50 g fresh flat leaf parsley

30 g fresh rosemary

50 g fresh chives

30 g fresh thyme

50 g fresh sage

100 g fresh breadcrumbs

2 tablespoons fennel seeds

2 cloves fresh garlic

zest and juice of 1 lemon

1 teaspoon sea salt

1 teaspoon crushed chilli

½ teaspoon black pepper

A good glug of olive oil to mix everything

Setup your barbecue for indirect cooking/ rotisserie, approximate temperature 170°C.

To make the filling, finely chop the herbs and garlic, add the remaining ingredients and mix in a bowl. Add enough olive oil to moisten the mixture: when the mixture is squeezed into a ball it should hold together, but still break apart when released. This will help keep the pork moist.

Take the pork and lay it flat, skin side up, on a board. Using a sharp blade, score the skin and sprinkle with salt. Turn the meat over so that it is skin side down. Butterfly the eye of the loin so that you have a large flat area. Pack the open meat with the stuffing mixture and roll up

tightly, so that the skin is left on the outside. Tie the whole thing together with butcher's twine or butchers elastic. (Refrigerate until ready to cook). Thread onto the rotisserie ensuring that it is tightly held. Put the pork into the barbecue and cook indirect rotisserie with a foil or baking tray underneath the meat.

Cook for around 2–3 hours (lid on) at between 180 and 200°C or until the pork is cooked. (You should look for an internal temperature in the centre of the loin of approximately 62°C.) To crisp up the crackling at the end, switch off the rotisserie with the skin facing the heat. Be careful not to let it burn.

Rest the pork for at least 15 minutes before removing the string and carving.

Maltese Pork Stew – Stuffat tal Majjal

This hearty, warming stew takes me back to my childhood. I always looked forward to helping my mum prepare and cook this dish, but not as much as I enjoyed eating it! These days I make it when I get a lot of trimmings from pork used on my barbecue classes. I smoke the trimmings before adding them to the pot for a little kiss of smoke.

500 g pork shoulder

500 g onions

500 g potatoes *(e.g. Maris Piper)*

300 g carrots

300 g leeks

200 g celery

4 cloves of garlic

1 litre chicken or beef stock

A small bunch of thyme

Salt and pepper to taste

Optional extras: you can also add a can of tomatoes and some frozen peas, or any other root vegetables of your choice.

Chop the pork and all of the vegetables, except the potatoes, into hearty sized chunks. Peel the potatoes and either leave whole or cut in half (depending on the size).

Put everything into a large saucepan, bring to the boil and reduce the heat to a gentle simmer. Simmer until all the vegetables are soft; the potatoes will have absorbed a lot of the juices.

Serve in a bowl with some buttered toasted bread for dipping.

The Grafty Gourmet Sausage

This is another of my award-winning sausage recipes, named after the village I used to live in (Grafty Green). It's a pure meat sausage with some unusual flavours, but it works. This is also a great sausage to hang and air dry or cold smoke, as long as you use a preservative.

1 kg pork shoulder and belly *(80% lean to 20% fat)*

250 g smoked bacon trimmings *(I used to use the trimmings from my homemade bacon)*

10 g salt

½ teaspoon of garlic powder

½ teaspoon cracked black pepper

½ teaspoon ground juniper berries

20 ml sherry vinegar

A pinch of ground cloves

1 teaspoon dried sage

1 teaspoon Angostura bitters

1 teaspoon light brown sugar

A pinch of ground mace

A pinch of hot chilli powder

A dash of Worcestershire sauce

1½ tablespoons bacon, goose or duck fat *(melted but cooled)*

Mince pork and bacon on coarse mince blade. Mix the dry ingredients together. Pour dry and wet ingredients onto pork in mixer and mix until well combined.

Mince the whole mixture again on medium mince blade. Leave overnight to allow flavours to infuse. Mix again before stuffing into sausage casings (I prefer natural hog casings for this).

Cold smoke/air dry (if Prague powder is used) or hot smoke fresh as desired.

||||||||||||||||||||||||||||||||||||||||||||||||||

Stuffed Double Pork Chop

I created this after being given some wonderful double pork loin chops. The little burst of fennel in the stuffing goes really well with the pork.

1 x 2 bone pork loin 'tomapork' chop

100 g chestnut mushrooms

½ a leek – white part only

50 g smoked streaky bacon

½ teaspoon salt

½ teaspoon ground black pepper

½ teaspoon fennel seeds

2 tablespoons chicken rub

Finely chop the mushrooms, leek and bacon and fry until cooked through and most of the moisture has evaporated. Add the salt, pepper and fennel seeds, mix through. Leave mixture to chill.

Using a sharp knife, make a pocket in the pork loin chop from the bone side (between the bones). Be careful not to go through or make holes.

Push the chilled filling into the pocket in the pork chop. Using some butcher's twine, tie the bones together, wrapping around the bottom ends of the bones to seal the pocket. Score the fat in a crisscross pattern. Sprinkle the outside of the meat on all sides with chicken rub, or a rub of your choice.

Cook over indirect heat at 140°C until the pork internal temperature measures 65°C (ensure you probe the pork meat, not the filling).

Either in a hot frying pan or directly over charcoal, place the pork on its fatty end and crisp up the fat covering. Before slicing, leave to rest for 15 minutes in a warm place.

Stuffed Pork Tenderloin

Years ago, I was asked by my old friend Dr BBQ (Ray Lampe) to come up with a recipe for his second book. This is one of the recipes I came up with for him. It seemed only right that I include it in my own book.

1 whole pork tenderloin

1 small red onion – finely chopped

125 g mushrooms – finely chopped

25 g butter or olive oil

Pinch of dried sage

Pinch of dried thyme

100 g fresh breadcrumbs

Grated rind of 1 lemon

2 tablespoons lemon juice

25 g toasted pine nut kernels

4 tablespoons fresh chopped parsley

3 teaspoons of sweet chilli sauce *(more if you like it hot)*

4 tablespoons fresh chopped coriander

100 g dried apricots – very finely chopped

Fresh spinach

Black pudding or sausage of your choice with skin removed

14 rashers of smoked streaky bacon

Fry the onion and mushrooms in the olive oil or butter until tender. Transfer to a bowl and add the sage, thyme, breadcrumbs, lemon rind, lemon juice, pine nut kernels, parsley, coriander and chilli sauce; mix well.

Take the pork tenderloin and butterfly it lengthways. Place a piece of cling film underneath it and another on top, then beat it out to an even thickness.

Remove the top piece of cling film, brush meat with butter and lay washed, de-stemmed spinach leaves so that the whole meat surface area is covered. Take the filling mix and spread it over the spinach – use your fingers to get an even covering.

Now take the diced black pudding or link sausage and mix with the chopped dried apricots. Lay it in the middle of the square along the length of the meat/stuffing area. Using the cling wrap to help you, roll the whole thing up tightly (similar to a Swiss roll or roulade).

Once rolled, wrap a bacon lattice around the whole piece of meat so that you have completely covered the meat. Roll up with cling film and refrigerate until ready to cook (best to leave this for around 1 hour to allow the flavours to infuse).

Cook over indirect heat at 150°C for approximately 1 hour or until a meat thermometer inserted into the centre reads 62°C. Allow meat to rest in a warm place for around 15 minutes and serve cut into approx. 1 cm slices.

Bourbon and Orange Glazed Ham

1 horseshoe gammon ham Joint *(you can use smoked or unsmoked)*

Glaze
250 g marmalade
100 g brown sugar
75 g whole grain mustard
50 g Bourbon
1 inch piece grated ground root
2 bird's eye chillies – finely chopped *(optional)*

24 hours before cooking – When barbecuing or baking a ham, it is always advisable to soak the joint in cold water (changing the water around every 2–3 hours) to remove excess saltiness.

On the day of cooking – Setup the barbecue to cook over indirect heat at 140°C.

Remove the joint from the soaking water and pat dry. Place on the barbecue, skin/fat side up and cook until the internal temperature measures 60°C.

Remove joint from the barbecue and remove the skin, leaving as much fat on the meat as possible.

Make the glaze by putting all the ingredients into a bowl and melting together in the microwave (or in a saucepan).

Using a sharp knife, score the fat (try not to cut into the meat) in a criss-cross pattern and brush the glaze gently over the fat. Return to the barbecue, raising the temperature to around 160°C.

Repeat the glazing process every 10 minutes until the glaze has been used up.

Check the internal temperature of the ham (it should be above 65°C) and remove from the barbecue.

Rest for an hour before carving. (If you want it hot, cover with a piece of parchment paper and foil, then place clean tea towels on top to keep the heat in.)

Carve into slices to serve.

The ham can be frozen either in chunks or in slices.

Raised Pork and Chicken Pie

I made this as part of my audition to a well-known baking competition. I really liked the pie and, having made a few of them, thought it would be good to share the recipe.

Hot water crust pastry

500 g plain flour, plus extra for dusting

125 g lard *(I like to use cold smoked lard)*

60 g butter

2 teaspoons salt

200 ml boiling water

1 egg, lightly beaten for glazing

Filling

400 g pork sausage meat

400 g pork loin – thinly sliced

200 g chicken breast – thinly sliced

100 g dried apricots – chopped

50 g pistachio nuts – roasted

Seasoning mix

2 teaspoons salt

1 teaspoon white pepper

1 tablespoon lemon thyme

1 teaspoon dried sage

½ teaspoon ground mace

½ teaspoon ground nutmeg

Jelly

6 gelatine leaves

300 ml good chicken stock

OR

1 pig trotter

500 ml water

1 carrot

1 onion

1 stick celery

To make the pastry, place the water, cubed lard and butter together in a saucepan. Bring to the boil and set aside whilst the fats melt. Place the flour and salt into a large bowl, make a well in the centre and pour in the water and fat mixture. Bring together to a smooth dough. Divide one third of the pastry off and wrap in cling film. Roll out the remaining dough into a large circle big enough to fully line a pre-greased 20 cm spring form cake tin, leaving some pastry overlapping the top of the tin.

Mix the seasoning ingredients together and sprinkle a little of the mix between each layer of the meats. Layer the filling as follows, ensuring you press the meat right into the edge of the pastry: half of the sausage meat, half of the pork loin, half of the apricots, half of the pistachios, all of the chicken, then the remaining pistachios, apricots, pork loin and sausage meat.

Roll out the remaining third of pastry and cover the whole pie with it, pushing it down at the edges to seal. Trim off any excess pastry and then crimp the edges. Brush with some of the beaten egg to glaze, make a 2 cm hole in the centre of the lid and raise the edges a little. This will allow the steam to escape, and the raised edges will help to stop the liquid flooding the pastry top. Decorate with leaves or a pattern of your choice. I like to create a rose of pastry to fit in the hole at the top when the pie is finished: this should be baked separately.

Bake in a pre-heated oven set to 180°C for 30 minutes, then turn the temperature down to 140°C and cook for a further 90 minutes, or until a food probe inserted through the hole in the centre and halfway into the meat reads 70°C. Remove from the oven. Turn the oven back up to 180°C, allow the pie to stand for 10 minutes and remove from the cake tin. Brush the sides of the pie with the remaining egg glaze and return to the oven for a further 15–20 minutes until the sides are golden brown. If the lid is starting to over-colour, place some foil over the top only.

While the pie is cooking, make the stock. I like to make a proper stock from a pig's trotter: the trotter contains enough natural gelatine to make a really good jelly. Place the trotter, cubed vegetables and water in a saucepan, bring to the boil and simmer for a couple of hours. Strain the liquid, place back in the pan and bring to the boil again. Boil until reduced by half, season with salt and pepper before leaving to cool.

If you're using chicken stock and gelatine, soak the gelatine in water until soft, place chicken stock in a saucepan and bring to a simmer. Drain the gelatine and squeeze out the excess water, then add to the stock and stir until it has dissolved. Leave to cool.

Once the pie is golden brown, remove from the oven and leave to cool. Once cold, pour the cooled stock into the pie through the hole in the top. Do this slowly allowing the liquid to disperse before adding more, until the pie is full. Chill again (preferably overnight) before serving.

You could also make this in a loaf tin if you prefer.

Smoky Brunswick Stew

This is my version of an Ol' Southern recipe. It's a great way to use up those bits of leftover barbecued meats – make a big pot, as it freezes well too!

500 g leftover barbecued chicken and pork	2 sticks celery
	1 red chilli
	250 g sweetcorn
300 ml chicken stock *(made from smoked chicken carcass and skin plus onion, carrot and celery)*	1 – 400 g tin of butter beans
	2 cloves of garlic
	½ teaspoon celery seed
450 g tin of chopped tomatoes	½ teaspoon ground cumin
1 large onion	Salt and pepper to taste

Make the chicken stock from 500 ml water, 1 onion quartered, 1 carrot, 1 stick celery and the carcass and skin of a smoked chicken – this is essential to give the stew its smoky flavour. Reduce the stock until you have 300 ml left.

Dice the onion, garlic and celery and finely chop the chilli (including seeds). Roughly chop the cooked meats.

Fry the onion and celery until softened. Add the chopped chicken, pork and chilli. Fry for 5 minutes.

Add the chicken stock and tomatoes. Simmer for 1 hour, stirring occasionally.

Add the butter beans and corn, then simmer for a further 30 minutes or until it has thickened. Season to taste with salt and pepper.

Serve in bowls with buttered, toasted sourdough bread on the side.

Baby Back Ribs

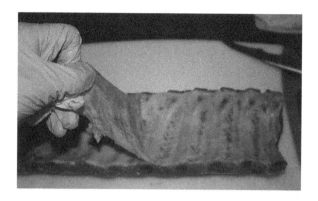

I really love a good meaty rack of baby back ribs: soft and sweet, with a little kick of spice. I like to use the rib rub recipe earlier in this book, but also to mix it up a little by layering some chicken rub with it.

Baby back ribs – leave racks whole

Rib rub

Barbecue sauce

First of all, look at the bone side of the ribs. They will usually have a silver skin or membrane over the bones. If it's there you should remove it. The reason for this is that the membrane doesn't cook down and will give a leathery texture to the back of the rib.

Allow 3 to 4 hours to cook your ribs. Prepare your smoker to cook over indirect heat – temperature around 140°C with some apple or whisky barrel wood.

Just before you're ready to cook, apply rub to both sides of the ribs and pat in gently; don't forget the tips of the bones. Don't leave the rub on the meat for longer than 30 minutes before putting into the smoker, bone side down. Cook for 2 hours.

Remove the ribs from the smoker and wrap (bone side up) with foil in a loose pouch with some liquid such as cider or apple juice. Seal the pouch to stop any steam escaping. Put back into the smoker for a further hour. Check the ribs are cooked by how soft they are: they should be pliable and bend easily without breaking. At this point open up the pouch and gently flip the ribs over so that they are bone side down. Coat with barbecue sauce and return to the smoker until the glaze is set and sticky (approximately 15 minutes).

Remove from the smoker and serve.

Bacon Wrapped Stuffing Log

Everything tastes great when it's wrapped in bacon: this is certainly no exception! I use this recipe for my Christmas stuffing, but it's a treat any time. Fill it with cheese and jalapenos, or breakfast ingredients… There's not much that you can't put in one of these bombs. Just use your imagination!

16 rashers of smoked streaky bacon

500 g good quality pork sausage meat

100 g dried cranberries

1 apple – finely diced

100 g chestnuts

1 tablespoon chopped fresh sage

1 teaspoon chopped fresh thyme

½ teaspoon salt

½ teaspoon pepper

On a piece of cling film, weave the bacon rashers into a lattice – it's really easy to do this, especially if you start from the middle.

Mix the sausage meat, cranberries, chestnuts, herbs, salt and pepper in a bowl. Tip out and make into a large sausage shape. Place in the centre of the bacon lattice: it should stretch almost the full width.

Roll the bacon around the meat. The ends should meet and overlap slightly. Tuck the bacon over the end. Roll the whole thing up tightly in cling film and leave in the fridge to set for at least 1 hour. This can be prepared the day before and refrigerated.

Cook indirectly in the barbecue at around 140°C for around 2 hours or until the internal temperature probes above 75°C.

Allow to rest for 15 minutes before cutting into slices.

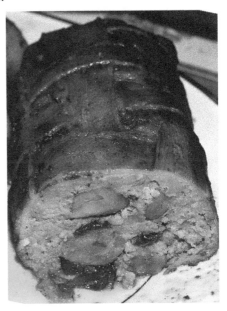

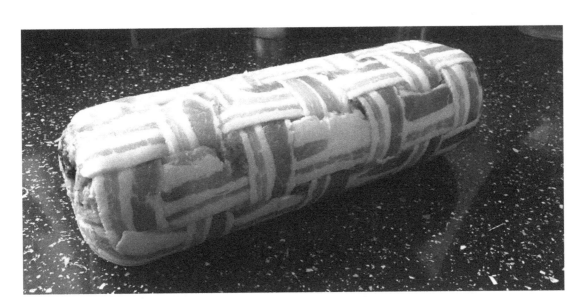

Korean Style Pork Shoulder Steaks

These are so tasty sliced up and served in taco shells or soft pancakes with a crunchy pickle slaw.

500 g boneless, skinless pork shoulder steaks *(around 2 cm thick)*

Spice Mix

100 g gochujang paste

100 g sweet mirin

100 g sake

50 g sunflower oil

6 fresh garlic cloves – crushed

2 tablespoons grated fresh ginger root

Mix the 'Spice Mix' in a large bowl. Add the pork steaks and work the spice mix into the meat, cover the bowl and leave to marinate in the fridge for around 4 hours or overnight if possible.

Set the barbecue to a temperature of approximately 140°C, indirect and place the pork onto the grill, using a piece of apple wood for flavour. Cook for approximately 1 hour.

To serve… Slice the pork thinly against the grain and pile into lightly toasted soft taco shells or soft pancakes, topped with some salad or American-style slaw.

Pulled Pork

Done properly, pulled pork can be a lovely way of eating pork shoulder. However, some of the supermarket variations have put a lot of people off. Try making it yourself: you'll become a convert!

4–5 kg pork shoulder joint with just the blade bone left in

Injection
100 g fine sea salt
100 g caster sugar
100 ml cider vinegar
500 ml water

Seasoning
Pork rub

The Soak
50 ml apple juice
50 ml cider vinegar
50 ml water

Take off as much fat as you can on the outside of the meat. If you leave too much fat on, it won't all render out and you'll end up removing the bark with the fat when you serve. There is plenty of internal fat to keep the meat moist and flavoured. You don't have to inject the meat; however, I find that it adds extra flavour right into the heart of the pork. Blend all injection ingredients until clear. Inject the meat with an injector of your choice. Do this in a pan and let it sit in the pan until time to season. Do this 4–8 hours before cooking.

Slash the top of the joint with some deep cuts. Apply your rub very liberally and rub (pat) in well, making sure you get it into the cuts, without packing it in.

Cook for 8 hours at 100°C with hickory, maple or apple wood. After 8 hours, transfer the pork to a pan and add the soak, cover with foil, then turn the temperature up to 140°C and cook for a further 4–6 hours. You want the meat to reach an internal temperature of around 98–102°C. Rest the pork for at least 1 hour in a warm place before pulling into the pan juices. When pulling, don't shred it into stringy pieces, you want to get nice lumps of pork that will retain their moisture.

I like a Carolina mustard sauce with my pork but go lightly so that the pork flavour comes through.

This is also lovely served with Lynchburg Candied Apples.

Home Cured Bacon

I used to make and sell bacon years ago when I had my farm. However, when I sold the farm I stopped making it. In the last couple of years, I've become less tolerant of the lack of flavour and abundance of liquid in shop-bought bacon and decided it was time to start making my own again. It was a good decision.

I haven't bought bacon for a long time. The only trouble with making great bacon is that your friends keep asking you to make some just for them!

Curing bacon at home can be quite simple, however you must be very strict about a few things.

Hygiene – make sure everything you use is clean and sterilised safely.

Measuring – ensure that when using nitrates to cure bacon, you measure precisely – an excess of nitrates can be poisonous.

Time – make sure you give the meat enough time to cure; you cannot rush bacon-making. Don't forget that if you want to leave the rind on, your bacon will take longer to cure.

Notes – Make notes of everything you do, weights of meat, before and after curing, amount of cure and other ingredients used, date you started curing, finished curing, left to form pellicle, smoked, equalised...in fact, everything should be noted to ensure that you retain a consistent product.

Cold Smoking – if you plan to cold smoke your bacon, ensure that you keep the temperature below 20°C – don't try cold smoking on a hot sunny day!

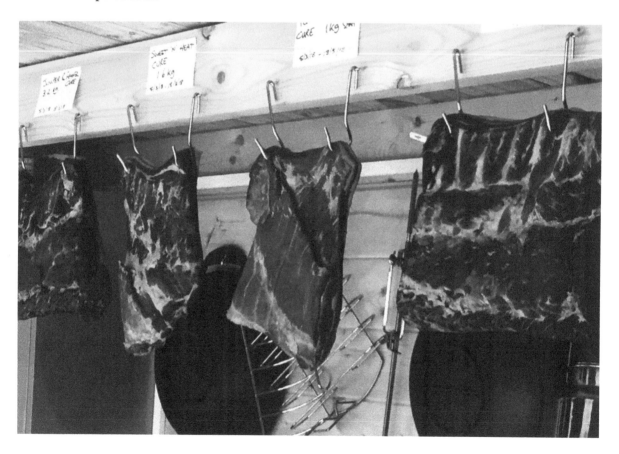

Slicing – If you're going to be making bacon regularly, I would advise you to invest in the best slicer that you can afford. A sharp knife will also do the job but won't give you a consistent slice.

Packing – Vacuum packing bacon into portions that you will easily use is the best way to preserve the best product possible. It will also keep the bacon nicely in the freezer and prevent freezer burn.

Label – Once you've packed your bacon, it is important to label it with the production date and type of cure used. If you're like me, you will have so many packs of different cured bacon in your freezer that there is no way you will remember which is which and when you made it.

Different Cuts of Bacon

Back is made from the pork loin, with the bones removed. I ask my butcher to leave about a 4 cm tail (as it leads to the belly) on the pork loin. I like to leave the cure on pork loin for 10 days before rinsing and drying.

Streaky is made from the pork belly, with the bones removed. I prefer to remove the rind and these timings are for a slab of belly without rind. I like to leave the cure on pork belly for 7 days before rinsing and drying.

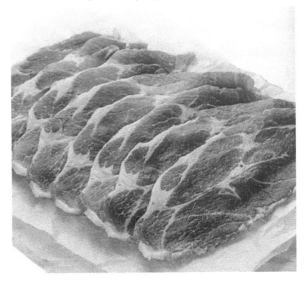

Collar is made from the pork shoulder/neck. This is an old-fashioned cut that due to its thickness takes even longer to cure. It consists of numerous small muscles and has a much stronger flavour.

I like to leave the cure on pork collar for 15 days before rinsing and drying.

How to Make Bacon

To make bacon, take your piece of meat and selected cure. Rub the meat with the cure so that it is fully covered. Either place in a vacuum bag and vacuum, then place in a zip lock bag, or leave in a non-reactive dish covered with cling film to cure. The meat should be cured in the fridge, preferably away from any other food. Turn the meat over, every day. Once the curing time has completed, remove the bacon from its bag or dish and rinse thoroughly in cold water. Pat dry with kitchen towel. Place on a non-reactive rack and return to the fridge to dry for two days.

To cold-smoke the bacon, I would recommend using a Cold Smoke Generator. ProQ Smokers supply a very good version of this, and I use mine all the time. Fill with dry wood dust – beech is a lovely wood to use on bacon, as is maple and hickory. Hang the bacon in your smoker and light the CSG as per the instructions. Leave to smoke for a full wood dust load (usually between 12 and 14 hours). Return to the fridge and leave for 24 hours. Smoke again if you wish, depending on how strong a smoke flavour you prefer. One or two smokes are usually my limit, as I enjoy a subtle flavour.

Once you have finished the smoking process, leave the bacon in the fridge for up to 1 week. (Wrap if the fridge is used for other things to prevent cross contamination.) At this point, it's time to slice and pack your bacon and to enjoy all your hard work.

Juniper, Fennel and Orange Bacon Cure

This is sufficient for a 2 kg piece of pork loin or belly.

30 g Supacure curing salt

50 g fine sea salt

40 g molasses sugar

5 g juniper berries – crushed in a pestle and mortar

2 g fennel seeds – crushed in a pestle and mortar

Fine zest of one orange

Maple, Coffee and Orange Bacon Cure

This is sufficient for a 2 kg piece of pork loin or belly.

150 g maple syrup

30 g Supacure curing salt

60 g fine sea salt

20 g dark brown sugar

20 g ground coffee

Fine zest of one orange

Pour maple syrup over pork loin and mix remaining ingredients in a bowl before rubbing onto the pork.

Molasses and Fennel Bacon Cure

This is sufficient for a 2 kg piece of pork loin or belly.

200 g dark molasses or treacle

30 g Supacure curing salt

60 g fine sea salt

20 g dark brown sugar

5 g fennel seeds – crushed in a pestle and mortar

Pour molasses over pork loin and mix remaining ingredients in a bowl before rubbing onto the pork.

Juniper Bacon Cure

This is sufficient for a 2 kg piece of pork loin or belly.

30 g Supacure curing salt

50 g fine sea salt

40 g molasses sugar

5 g juniper berries – crushed in a pestle and mortar

MEAT: LAMB

Smoked Rack of Lamb with Pumpkin and Feta

I love the simplicity of a lightly smoked rack of lamb and having grown quite a few pumpkins found that this paired with it really well.

1 lamb rack
½ pumpkin
100 g feta cheese
Olive oil

1 pomegranate
Salt
Pepper

Trim the lamb rack and score the fat into a diamond pattern season with salt and pepper. Place fat side down into a frying pan and sear the fat side only until it starts to crisp up. Remove from the pan.

Cut the pumpkin into long wedges and peel them. Season the pumpkin wedges with salt and drizzle with some olive oil before roasting them in the smoker until tender (approx. one hour at 150°C).

Put the lamb rack into the smoker with the pumpkin and cook until the internal temperature measures 55°C. Remove from the smoker and rest in a warm place.

To assemble the dish, pile the pumpkin wedges on a plate, cut the lamb rack into cutlets and place with the pumpkin. Either cube or crumble the feta cheese over the top, sprinkle with pomegranate seeds and drizzle with a little olive oil.

Dukkah and Apricot Stuffed Leg of Lamb

Lamb is always a great alternative on the barbecue and you can do so much with it.

This recipe makes great use of the Dukkah recipe earlier in the book and gives the lamb a wonderfully sweet smoky flavour.

1 leg of lamb, bone removed

Stuffing
150 g dried apricots – roughly chopped

250 g luxury Dukkah mix
Sat and pepper to taste
Olive oil

Chop the apricots and mix with the Dukkah to form the stuffing. Remove the bone from the leg of lamb butterfly and lay out flat, drizzle with a little olive oil.

Press the stuffing into the leg of lamb leaving a border around the edges, sprinkle with a little salt and pepper, then roll tightly and tie with butcher's twine. Rub the outside of the meat with olive oil and season with more salt and pepper.

Prepare the smoker (indirect) with a chunk of fruitwood of your choice and place the lamb in the smoker. Cook at 140°C for 3-4 hours, or until the meat is tender.

This also works really well on a rotisserie.

Rest in a warm place for 30 minutes before slicing to serve.

Middle Eastern Crusted Lamb Shoulder – Sharing Platter

Heat the barbecue with indirect setup to 180°C.

Put the lamb into the barbecue with a chunk of wood of your choice for flavour and cook for 2 hours.

After 2 hours, place the lamb into a pan with 500 ml cherry juice. Cover with foil and continue to cook for a further 3 hours. The lamb should be soft and easy to remove from the bone. Leave to rest for 30 minutes.

During the last half hour of the cook, smoke the beetroot (I tend to use pre-cooked beetroot and smoke to heat it and add flavour).

Shred the lamb and place on a large board. Randomly place the smoked beetroot (cut into wedges), cubed feta, halved dates, coriander and pomegranate seeds over the lamb.

Mix yoghurt and harissa together. Serve in a bowl next to the lamb platter.

1 lamb shoulder – bone in

Crust
1 onion
2 teaspoons coriander seeds
1 teaspoon cumin seeds
1 tablespoon olive oil
Small bunch of coriander stalks *(reserve leaves)*
4 cloves of garlic
Zest and juice of one lemon
1 tablespoon instant coffee

500 ml cherry juice

To Serve
250 g smoked beetroot – cut into wedges
200 G fresh dates – pitted and halved
100 G pomegranate seeds
200 G feta cheese – cubed
Coriander leaves – torn

Dressing/Sauce
100 ml Natural yoghurt
2 tablespoons harissa paste

Place all of the crust ingredients into a blender and blend until they form a paste.

Slash the lamb on both sides and spread the paste over both sides of the lamb shoulder. Leave to marinate for a couple of hours or overnight, covered in the fridge.

Flatbreads

350 g self-raising flour *(more if needed)*
350 g plain yoghurt
1 teaspoon chilli flakes *(optional)*

Chopped coriander *(or herb of your choice)*
Salt and pepper

Mix all of the flatbread ingredients together until you have a fairly smooth dough; add more flour if needed. Set aside for 30 minutes to rest.

Take balls of the dough, flour well and roll into flat discs.

Cook on a rack or plancha over direct heat until the bread bubbles up. Flip over and cook on the other side: it should still be soft and pliable.

Smoked Spiced Lamb Shanks

Serve on a bed of fried leeks and cabbage with smoky Hassleback potatoes.

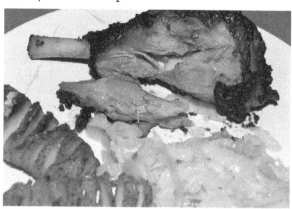

I've always loved braised lamb shanks, so decided to try them slowly smoked over oak, the result was wonderful!

4 lamb shanks

Marinade
3 tablespoons olive oil

Juice of one fresh lemon

2 tablespoons light soy sauce

1½ tablespoons coarse ground black pepper

1½ tablespoons flaked sea salt

1 tablespoon garlic granules

1 tablespoon smoked paprika

1 teaspoon dried thyme

1 teaspoon dried rosemary

1 teaspoon ground ginger

1 teaspoon turmeric

½ teaspoon ground cumin

Add all of the marinade ingredients into a blender and blend into a paste.

Make cuts into the meat of the lamb shanks (this helps the marinade penetrate deeper). Place the four lamb shanks into a Ziplock bag and pour in the marinade paste. Rub the marinade into the lamb shanks and place in the fridge overnight (or for up to 24 hours).

Heat the smoker to around 150°C, using the indirect method with a lump of cherry wood for flavour.

Smoke for around 4–5 hours or until the lamb is tender and almost falling off the bone.

Minty Lamb and Pea Burgers

These make a great spring/summer burger: they're light, fresh and very tasty.

500 g lamb mince

2 tablespoon mint sauce

2 tablespoon mint jelly

200 g frozen peas – cooked and mashed

1 tablespoon salt

1 tablespoon ground black pepper

Mix all ingredients together thoroughly and form into 4 x 125 g patties. Leave in fridge to firm up.

Cook over a high indirect heat for around 3-4 minutes per side, turning once.

Serve in a bun of your choice with lettuce, cucumber and feta salsa and minty sour cream dressing.

Minty Sour Cream Dressing

50 ml sour cream

1 tablespoon mint sauce
(not jelly)

Salt and pepper to taste

Mix both ingredients together and spread on the base of a burger bun, top with lettuce, burger, salsa and a little more dressing.

Cucumber and Feta Salsa

½ cucumber

1 large tomato – peeled and deseeded

100 g feta cheese

1 tablespoon fresh mint – chopped

1 tablespoon fresh flat leaf parsley – chopped

1 tablespoon olive oil

1 tablespoon lemon juice

Salt and pepper to taste

Peel and deseed the cucumber and tomato, chop all ingredients into small dice and mix together with the oil and lemon juice.

|||||||||||||||||||||||||||||||||||||||||||||||||||||||

Reverse Seared Kangaroo Rump Steak

I asked my butcher for something unusual, he told me to 'hop it' and sent me kangaroo rump steak. I hadn't realised what a versatile, tasty meat this was and was quite happy with the results.

4 kangaroo rump steaks

Marinade

6 juniper berries – crushed

1/2 teaspoon salt

Zest and juice of half an orange

1 tablespoon fresh rosemary – chopped

1 teaspoon coarse black pepper

100 ml olive oil

50 ml red wine vinegar

Sauce

2 tablespoons redcurrant jelly

8 tablespoons port (or red wine)

Pomegranate seeds

Mix all of the marinade ingredients together, place in a zip lock bag and add the kangaroo rump steaks. Leave overnight.

Set your barbecue to indirect heat at as low a temperature as you can get it, I got mine to 75°C for this. Place the steaks into the barbecue and smoke for one hour. Remove and set on a plate while you crank up the heat for direct grilling. Sear the steaks for 2-3 minutes per side to finish cooking and give you a good crust. They need to be cooked no more than medium-rare or they will become very tough. Set aside in a warm place to rest.

Put the port and redcurrant jelly into a small pan, bring to the boil and reduce until it has turned thick and syrupy. Serve the steaks drizzled with the sauce and sprinkled with pomegranate seeds.

Moroccan Pulled Lamb with an Orange and Carrot Salad

There's something wonderful about lamb shoulder. Its high fat content helps it to stay moist. Pairing it with the sweet acidity of this salad and bundling it into a flatbread, you have a wonderful, fresh-tasting dish.

1 whole shoulder of lamb, bone in
Olive oil

Ras-el-Hanout Seasoning
1 teaspoon salt
1 teaspoon ground cumin
1 teaspoon ground ginger
¾ teaspoon ground black pepper
½ teaspoon ground coriander seeds
½ teaspoon ground cinnamon
½ teaspoon ground allspice
½ teaspoon paprika
½ teaspoon turmeric
¼ teaspoon ground cloves

Salad
2 oranges, segmented
2 carrots
1 pomegranate

Flatbread
300 g self-raising flour
300 ml plain yoghurt
Pinch of salt and pepper

Dressing
150 g plain yoghurt
1 tablespoon harissa paste

Set your smoker to indirect heat at 140°C: add wood of your choice. Mix all the spices together. Rub the lamb shoulder with a little olive oil and cover evenly with the ras-el-hanout. Cook for around six hours or until very tender (the bone should pull out easily). Remove from the smoker and leave to rest for 30 minutes before pulling into a nice size shred.

Peel and segment the oranges, peel the carrots and using a vegetable peeler, slice into long thin strips. Mix the orange, carrot and pomegranate seeds together and leave to one side.

To make the flatbreads, mix the flour, salt, pepper and yoghurt into a smooth dough, shape into small balls and roll out into small round thin discs (around the size of a CD). Cook the flatbreads either in a hot frying pan or over a hot charcoal fire, flip over to cook both sides.

To serve, pile flatbreads with pulled lamb, add a little of the salad and top with the harissa dressing.

VEGETABLE DISHES

Butternut Squash, Feta, Mixed Seeds and Pomegranate Salad

Smoked Beet Wellington

When my family come to visit, I like to create similar dishes for everyone, including my vegetarian niece, Alice. So whilst the rest of us were tucking into Beef Wellington, she got to enjoy my Beet Wellington.

A hearty salad, packed with flavour and texture.

1 butternut squash	25 g sunflower seeds
½ teaspoon salt	80 g pomegranate seeds
½ teaspoon black pepper	2 tablespoons chopped fresh parsley
50 ml olive oil	2 tablespoons chopped fresh coriander
200 g feta cheese	
1 lime – juice and zest	1 long red Dutch chilli
50 ml olive oil	20 g mixed leaves
25 g pumpkin seeds	10 ml French dressing

Smoke the pumpkin and sunflower seeds for around 1 hour at 80°C. Cool. (You can make lots of this and store it in an airtight container for future use.)

Peel, de-seed and dice the squash into 2 cm cubes, toss with olive oil and salt and pepper place in a baking tray and roast in the barbecue at 150°C for 30–40 minutes or until tender but with a little bite. Leave to cool.

Cut the feta into small dice, deseed the chilli, finely slice and mix with the remaining ingredients. Lightly toss with the squash.

Serve piled high on a bed of mixed leaves.

This salad is also lovely served rolled in a wrap with some lettuce and ranch dressing.

500 g fresh raw beetroot (of similar size)	1 teaspoon salt
100 g shallots	1 teaspoon black pepper
100 g wild mushrooms	100 g goat's cheese
2 cloves garlic	4 sprigs lemon thyme
	500 g puff pastry

Place the beetroot in your smoker at a temperature around 150°C and cook for between 1 and 2 hours until the beetroot are tender. Remove and peel.

Whilst the beets are cooking, finely dice the shallots, garlic and mushrooms. Fry the shallots until soft, add the garlic and mushrooms and continue to fry until all of the moisture has gone. Remove from the heat, add the finely chopped lemon thyme, salt and pepper, mix well and leave to cool.

Roll out the puff pastry, spread the cooled shallot and mushroom mix over two-thirds of the pastry (but not to the edge). Top with the goat's cheese. Trim the beetroots to sit side by side in a log form and roll the pastry up so that the beetroot is covered by the shallot mix and the cheese. Shape the pastry into a log and seal at each end, tucking any edges underneath. Brush with beaten egg and use the back of a knife to create a pattern on the pastry (be careful not to cut through the pastry).

Either bake in a pre-heated oven at 180°C (or return to the barbecue at 180°C) for approximately 30–40 minutes until the pastry is cooked through and golden brown.

Serve in thick slices.

||||||||||||||||||||||||||||||||||||||||||||||||||

Ratatouille

I love to grow my own fresh vegetables. Sometimes they're quite abundant, and this is my go-to dish to make ahead of time and freeze so that I can enjoy food from my garden all year around.

1 marrow

2 peppers *(red or green)* – sliced

2 red onions – sliced

12 fresh tomatoes *(or 1 tin)*

2 fresh chillies – sliced *(I use jalapenos)*

50 ml red wine

1 stock cube *(I prefer beef, but you can use vegetable)*

Salt and pepper to taste

Slice the marrow into 2 mm thick slices. Cook on your barbecue over direct heat or in a frying pan until softened.

Fry the onions, jalapenos and peppers until soft. Add the cooked marrow slices. Skin the tomatoes, roughly chop and add to the pan. Simmer gently until everything is soft and the sauce has thickened.

Season with salt and pepper and serve over pasta, rice or as a side dish.

Middle Eastern Style Spiced Cauliflower Platter

I love to serve this dish alongside its lamb counterpart, so that vegetarians and carnivores can feast together.

1 or 2 cauliflowers (depending on size) divided into florets *(you can also use Romanesco broccoli)*

4 tablespoons sunflower oil

4 tablespoons water

2 tablespoons ras al hanout

1–2 tablespoons harissa paste *(to taste)*

2 tablespoons maple syrup

Chopped coriander stalks *(save the leaves for serving)*

Sea salt

To Serve

Cubed feta cheese

Pomegranate seeds

Dates

Coriander leaves

Dressing

100 g Greek-style yoghurt

20 g Harissa paste

Mix the marinade ingredients together until well blended.

Put the cauliflower in a heatproof dish, pour the marinade over the cauliflower and coat in the marinade.

Place in the barbecue at around 140–160°C – indirect heat.

Cook until a knife slides in easily and the cauliflower is slightly caramelised (or until cooked to your liking) – this will take between 30 minutes and an hour.

Serve on a board topped with cubed feta cheese, pomegranate seeds, chopped dates and coriander leaves.

|||||||||||||||||||||||||||||||||||||||||||||||||||||||

Stuffed Butternut Squash

This was one of our Meat Free Christmas Specials at our restaurant but there's no reason why it can't be enjoyed any time. Makes a great sharing side dish too.

1 Butternut Squash *(choose nicely shaped ones)*

75 g quinoa *(red and white mixed)*

Vegetable stock made with 150 ml water

1 onion

½ red pepper

½ green pepper

75 g chopped chestnuts

75 g grated parsnip

75 g grated carrot

25 g Craisins *(dried cranberries)*

pinch of salt and pepper

Topping

20 g toasted pine nuts

20 g toasted pumpkin seeds

50 g crumbled feta cheese

Cut the butternut squash in half (lengthwise) and scoop out the seeds. Score the flesh with a diagonal pattern, being careful not to cut through the skin or the edges. Drizzle with oil, sprinkle with salt and pepper. Place in the smoker for 2–3 hours at 140°C or until just soft.

When cooked, scoop out any thicker areas of the squash, leaving around ½ cm of flesh on the skin… Again, make sure you don't damage the skin or shape of the squash.

While the butternut squashes are smoking, simmer the quinoa, vegetable stock and water in a saucepan until softened, drain and leave to one side.

In a pan, fry the finely diced onion until soft and caramelised. Add the peppers and continue to cook for a couple of minutes. Add the grated carrot, grated parsnip, cooked quinoa, chestnuts, Craisins, salt and lemon pepper. Continue to cook for a few more minutes until everything is combined.

Fill the hollowed-out butternut squash with the mixture and return to the smoker until everything is heated through.

Just before serving sprinkle with mixture of crumbled feta cheese, smoked pine nuts and pumpkin seeds.

||||||||||||||||||||||||||||||||||||||||||||||||||||

Smoked Ricotta and Pea Ravioli

I love making ravioli! Smoking the ricotta gives a nice, subtly different flavour which works really well with the sweetness of the peas.

Pasta	Filling
3 large eggs	1 tub ricotta
300 g type 00 flour	Zest of ½ a lemon
	100 g petit pois, mashed
	Salt and pepper

Pesto Sauce
50 g rocket
50 g petit pois
50 g fresh coriander
20 g toasted pine nut

25 ml extra virgin olive oil
20 g Parmesan cheese
Salt and pepper
Extra Parmesan shavings to garnish

Make the pasta by mixing the eggs and flour into a dough. Knead until smooth and rest for 20 minutes.

Place ricotta in a bowl and cover with cling film. Using a smoking gun, blow smoke into the bowl. Reseal and leave to stand for 15 minutes before adding the lemon zest, mashed petit pois, salt and pepper. Mix well.

Roll the pasta to very thin sheets, place dessertspoon-sized blobs of the filling at intervals, cover with a second sheet, press out any air, seal and cut into rounds.

Make the sauce by placing all of the ingredients into a blender and blending to a pesto-like consistency. Season to taste.

Cook the pasta in gently boiling water for 2–3 minutes, drain well and serve drizzled with the pesto sauce and shavings of Parmesan cheese.

Cheesy, Mac and Cheese

Not your everyday mac 'n' cheese, but sometimes you just need to go big!

500 g dried penne pasta

50 g butter

50 g plain flour

500 ml milk

2 tablespoons whole grain mustard

350 g cheese of your choice – grated *(I like to use a mix of Cheddar, Red Leicester, Double Gloucester and mozzarella)*

250 g Brie or Camembert – torn into cubes

To Finish

50 g butter

100 g panko breadcrumbs

Cook the pasta in a large pan of salted boiling water until just cooked, drain and return to the pan.

Melt butter in a saucepan over a medium heat, mix in the flour and cook until the mixture is bubbling and starts to foam. Whisk in the milk a little at a time until incorporated and there are no lumps: the mixture should be the consistency of single cream. Whisk in the mustard and remove from the heat. Stir the grated cheese into the sauce. Add the cheese sauce to the pasta and mix well. Pour half of the cheesy mix into a baking pan and top with the cubed Brie or Camembert before pouring the remaining mix over it. Melt the 50 g butter in a frying pan and stir in the panko breadcrumbs. Mix until the crumbs are coated in the butter, then scatter the buttery crumbs over the mac 'n' cheese.

Put into barbecue and cook at around 150°C for around 30 minutes or until bubbling and browned on top. Don't leave it too long, or the pasta will soak up the sauce and it won't be lovely and soft and gooey. Serve immediately.

|||||||||||||||||||||||||||||||||||||||||||||||||||||||||

Black Bean Burger

Healthy, herby and tasty: what more could you want in a veggie burger?

1 tablespoon rapeseed oil

1 large egg

1 can black beans, rinsed and drained

50 g panko breadcrumbs

3 finely chopped spring onions

2 tablespoons chopped fresh coriander

¾ teaspoon ground cumin

¼ teaspoon salt

¼ teaspoon chilli

1 garlic clove, minced

Place oil, egg and black beans in a food processor. Pulse 20 times or until mixture becomes a coarsely chopped paste. Combine bean mixture, panko, onions and remaining ingredients in a bowl.

Divide bean mixture into four equal portions. Shape each into a ¾-inch-thick patty.

Heat a non-stick pan or flattop grill over medium-high heat, brush with oil and cook burgers for around 3–4 minutes on each side, until nicely crusted

Serve each burger with a soft fried egg (optional).

Root Burger Topped with Feta and Orange Salad

This earthiness of this burger is complemented by the freshness of the orange and feta salad.

2 large raw beetroot

200 g quinoa

2 large parsnips, grated

2 large carrots, grated

1 large onion, very finely chopped

300 g medium oatmeal

½ teaspoon dried sage

1 level teaspoon ground black pepper

2 level teaspoons salt

Smoke the whole, peeled beetroot until cooked but still slightly firm. Allow to cool. Grate and squeeze out as much moisture as you can.

Boil the quinoa for 10 minutes covered with a lid. Remove the saucepan from the heat and leave to sit, covered, until cool. Drain to remove excess water.

Fry the onions until soft and slightly caramelised. Leave to cool.

In large bowl, add the grated vegetables, onions, herbs and seasonings. When the quinoa has cooled down, add to the bowl. Add 300 g oatmeal and mix by hand, keep adding oatmeal until the mixture is firm enough to hold together. Taste and adjust seasoning if needed.

Divide the mixture into approx. 250 g sized burgers and place on a tray. Refrigerate and leave to rest for a while to firm up. Cook on a hot grill until heated through with a light crust on each side.

Feta and Orange Salad

100 g feta cheese – crumbled

1 orange, segmented

20 g dried cranberries

French dressing

Crumble some feta, segment some oranges and mix together with some dried cranberries. Toss lightly in a simple French dressing. Put salad in a small dish on a bed of shredded lettuce and serve on top of the burger (or on the side).

Lentil Barley Burgers

Healthy, hearty and really filling!

125 g dried green lentils – cooked with ½ litre of vegetable stock

100 g dried pearl barley – cooked with ½ litre vegetable stock

1 small finely chopped onion

1 small, grated carrot

1 small, grated parsnip

50 g green beans – finely chopped

2 cloves finely chopped garlic

1½ tablespoons tomato paste

½ teaspoon caster sugar

1 teaspoon ground cumin

A pinch of dried thyme

½ teaspoon chipotle chili paste

½ teaspoon of salt

125 g dried breadcrumbs

½ tablespoon American mustard

1 teaspoon finely chopped fresh parsley

½ teaspoon freshly ground black pepper

Combine vegetable stock and lentils in a saucepan; bring to a boil. Cover, reduce heat and simmer until lentils are tender. Combine vegetable stock and pearl barley in a saucepan; bring to a boil. Cover, reduce heat and simmer until barley is tender, drain well. Place lentils and barley in a large bowl, using stick blender, roughly blend leaving some barley and lentils whole.

Heat a pan over medium-high heat. Add a little oil, onion and carrot; fry until tender, stirring occasionally. Add garlic; cook for 1 minute, stirring constantly. Add tomato paste, sugar, cumin, thyme, chipotle chili paste and salt; cook for 5 minutes, stirring constantly.

Add onion mixture to lentils along with another pinch of salt, barley and remaining ingredients and mix well, add more breadcrumbs if necessary. Check seasoning and add more if needed. Cover and refrigerate for 1 hour or until firm. Divide mixture into six equal portions, shaping each into a burger patty.

To cook: grill on the barbecue or cook in a frying pan for at least 6 minutes or until heated through. The sides should be golden brown and a light crust should have formed.

Serve in a toasted Brioche bun with your choice of burger trimmings.

||||||||||||||||||||||||||||||||||||||||||||||||||||||||

Quinoa and Fennel Salad

2 fennel bulbs – stalks removed

4 tablespoons fresh flat leaf parsley

2 tablespoons fresh coriander

2 tablespoons fresh mint

1 tablespoon fresh dill

2 limes – zest from one and juice from both

100 g dried cranberries

½ head of celery

2 cups of quinoa

30 g butter

1½ teaspoons ground cumin

Pinch of salt

20 g mixed leaves

10 ml of French dressing

Slice the fennel wafer-thin. Keep one bulb raw and sauté the other in olive oil, tossing in a little butter at the last minute. Chill.

Soak the dried cranberries in hot water for 10 minutes to rehydrate them.

Finely chop all the herbs and finely slice the celery.

Cook the quinoa in salted boiling water until tender with a little bite and refresh in cold water before draining thoroughly.

Toss all the ingredients together with the limejuice and zest and a little seasoning. Serve on some dressed mixed leaves.

Beetroot, Orange and Pecan Salad

1 kg raw beetroot

2 tablespoons demerara sugar

1 tablespoon salt

50 ml olive oil

pinch lemon pepper

50 g toasted pecans

1 orange – zest and segments

20 g mixed leaves

Dressing

10 g capers – chopped

Pinch of salt

Pinch of pepper

25 ml cider vinegar

1 teaspoon whole grain mustard

25 ml olive oil

Dill to garnish

Peel and dice the beetroot into 1 cm cubes, sprinkle with salt, lemon pepper, orange zest, demerara sugar, toss with olive oil and smoke at 120°C for 45 minutes, then roast at 180°C for a further 45 minutes until tender but still with a little bite.

For the dressing, drain and finely chop the capers, add the mustard, olive oil and salt and pepper and mix thoroughly.

To serve, toss the cooked beetroot, segmented orange and mixed leaves with the dressing and serve with some torn dill leaves to garnish.

Honey Smoked Beetroot Sliders

Tender slices of smoked beetroot, sweetened with honey and served in a slider bun.

650 g large cooked beetroot *(not in vinegar)*

2 tablespoons fresh thyme, finely chopped

2 tablespoons balsamic vinegar

2 tablespoons light olive oil

2 tablespoons honey

Salt and pepper to taste

Slider-sized brioche buns

Lamb's lettuce

Horseradish sauce

Cut each beetroot into 1 cm slices (they should be the same diameter as the 'slider' buns), season and toss with the other ingredients until coated. Sprinkle with salt and pepper.

Arrange on a tray and place onto shelf of smoker and cook for 30 minutes at 160°C, turning once halfway through cooking, until the beetroot is sticky and glazed.

Serve in 'slider' buns with lamb's lettuce and horseradish sauce and a garnish.

Butternut Squash Falafel

These are a lovely variation on a traditional falafel, with lots of flavour and a softer texture.

400 g butternut squash

1½ tablespoons oil

2 shallots finely diced

2 cloves garlic crushed

1 teaspoon ground cumin

1 teaspoon ground coriander

½ teaspoon chilli powder

400 g can chickpeas, drained and rinsed

3 tablespoons coriander leaves, chopped

3 tablespoons parsley leaves, chopped

2 tablespoons breadcrumbs

Cube the butternut squash and roast in either a barbecue or an oven at 180°C until tender.

Fry the shallots in a little oil until soft. Add the garlic and spices, cook for a couple of minutes and leave to cool.

Place the drained chickpeas in a food processor and pulse a few times until broken up but still chunky.

Place roasted butternut squash in a bowl and mash with a fork until you have a rough purée. Add the chickpeas, shallot mix and herbs and gram flour. Season well and mix until everything is combined.

Shape into balls and flatten slightly. Set in the fridge for around 30 minutes.

Cook on a plancha or on a baking sheet set over the grills. A piece of apple wood will complement the falafels.

Serve with watercress salsa verde.

Watercress Salsa Verde

100 g watercress

Small bunch of parsley

Small handful of mint leaves

2 spring onions

2 teaspoons Dijon mustard

1 garlic clove

8 tablespoons extra virgin olive oil

Juice of one lemon

2 tablespoons capers

Salt and pepper to taste

Put everything into a blender – with the garlic, capers and spring onions at the bottom – and blend until you get the consistency you want. (This can be served smooth or chunky.)

SWEET TREATS AND SAVOURY BAKES

Chocolate Chunk Cheesecake

A great finish to any barbecue: not too sweet, with a lovely fresh fruit finish.

Base
200 g digestive biscuits
75 g salted pretzels
50 g dark chocolate chips
75 g melted butter

Cheesecake mix
2 x 300 g tubs of full fat cream cheese
4 eggs
200 g caster sugar

1 tablespoon vanilla extract
50 ml Greek yoghurt
100 g white chocolate – chopped into chunks
100 g milk chocolate – chopped into chunks

Topping
200 g fresh raspberries
200 g fresh blueberries
100 g white chocolate
100 g double cream

Crush the digestive biscuits and pretzels together to form a crumb and mix in the chocolate chips. Melt the butter and add the melted butter to the crumb and chocolate. Mix until well combined. Line the base of a 23 cm round spring-form baking tin and butter the base and the sides. Press the crumb mix into the bottom of the tin and press well. Bake in a pre-heated oven (170°C) for 15 minutes. Remove from the oven and leave to one side to cool. Turn the oven down to 160°C.

In a large bowl, combine cream cheese, eggs, sugar, vanilla and yoghurt – whisk until smooth. Fold in the chocolate chunks and pour the mix onto the baked biscuit base.

Place in the oven and bake for 45 minutes to 1 hour. To check it's cooked, just wobble the baking tin, there should be just a little movement in the middle. Close the oven door, turn the oven off and leave the cheesecake in the oven to cool – this will take a few hours but this process should prevent the top of the cheesecake from cracking.

After 4–5 hours, remove the cheesecake from the oven, cover loosely and place in the fridge to finish cooling, overnight preferably.

In a small pan, heat the double cream until it almost comes to the boil. Remove from the heat, add the chopped white chocolate and stir until it melts. Leave to cool for around an hour, stirring occasionally.

Pour the white chocolate sauce over the top of the cold cheesecake (the sides will be slightly raised so the sauce should sit in a pool in the middle). Leave a little sauce for a final decoration. Arrange the raspberries and blueberries over the top of the cheesecake and drizzle with a little more sauce, before returning to the fridge to set.

Cut into wedges to serve, with a drizzle of double cream or honey Greek yoghurt.

Crispy Fried Banana Wraps

Simple, deep fried and just sooo good!

2 fresh firm bananas

16 wonton wrappers

1 teaspoon cinnamon

3 tablespoons icing sugar

Sieve the icing sugar and cinnamon into a small bowl. Peel the bananas, top and tail them and cut in half. Stand them on their end and then cut into quarters. You should be left with 16 quarters of banana each around 70 cm long. Sprinkle the bananas with the icing sugar and cinnamon mix.

Brush a little water around the edges of the wonton wrapper and fold in the edges over the banana before tightly rolling the wrap. Ensure all edges are sealed.

Deep fry at 170°C until the wontons are golden and crispy. Drain and sprinkle with more of the cinnamon sugar mix.

Eat whilst still hot and crunchy.

Lemon Curd

Sharp, yet sweet. This curd is lovely on toast or injected into doughnuts or cupcakes.

275 ml freshly squeezed lemon juice – strained

250 g sugar

4 whole eggs

4 egg yolks

200 g unsalted butter

1 teaspoon salt

Wash jars and place upside down into an oven. Turn on oven to 110°C, leave for 5 minutes and turn off oven…leave jars in oven whilst you are making the curd. In a bowl, whisk the eggs, sugar and salt together until smooth. Add lemon juice and continue to whisk until incorporated. Place the bowl above a saucepan of simmering water (i.e. making a double boiler). Stir continuously until the mixture thickens and coats the back of a spoon thickly. Turn off heat, cut butter into cubes and stir into lemon mix. When fully melted, whisk once more to ensure it is incorporated. Ladle into hot sterilised jars, put a disk of waxed paper on top and screw on lid. Refrigerate.

Lemon-Blueberry Mini Cheesecakes Recipe

These are a great little barbecue party dessert – easy to serve, as people get their own little cheesecake!

16 digestive biscuits

100 g butter, melted

600 g full fat cream cheese

200 g caster sugar

4 eggs

2 teaspoons vanilla extract

Grated zest of two lemons

200 g fresh or frozen blueberries

50 caster sugar

Heat oven to 180°C. In a medium size pan, melt the butter. Crush digestive biscuits in a plastic bag with a rolling pin. Add to butter and mix well until coated.

Place cupcake liners in a muffin tin. Add around a tablespoon of crumb mixture into each cupcake liner. Using your fingers, squash the crumbs down and along the sides of the cupcake liners. Bake for about 10 minutes. Allow to cool and set aside.

Place cream cheese and sugar into a large mixing bowl. Using an electric mixer, beat until fluffy and light. Add eggs and vanilla extract and lemon zest, beat until thoroughly combined. Divide the cheesecake batter into cupcake liners equally and drop 4 blueberries on top of each, pushing them down into the batter. Bake for 20 to 25 minutes. Allow to cool on a cooling rack for at least 15 to 20 minutes. Remove from cupcake tin.

Place remaining blueberries into a saucepan with 50 g sugar and bring to the boil. Cook until thickened, then set aside to cool.

Refrigerate for at least 4 hours or overnight. Remove from cupcake liners before serving. Just before serving place a teaspoon of the 'blueberry jam' on top of each cheesecake.

Peach and Blueberry Cobbler

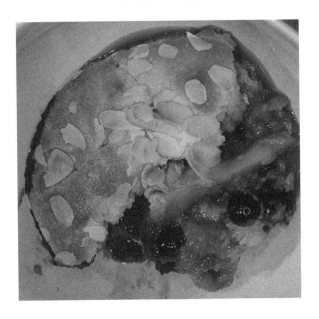

Full of fruit with a gooey, chewy cobbler topping... this makes a great barbecue dessert and can be cooked from scratch on the barbecue.

8 fresh peaches, peeled, halved and de-stoned *(you can cheat and use canned peaches)*

200 g fresh blueberries

75 g caster sugar

75 g light brown sugar

Juice from half a lemon

½ teaspoon cinnamon

Pinch of fresh grated nutmeg

For the topping

250 g plain flour

150 g light brown sugar

100 g butter

1 teaspoon baking powder

Pinch of salt

100 ml buttermilk

3 tablespoons demerara sugar

50 g flaked almonds

1 teaspoon ground cinnamon

Slice each of the peaches into two rounds and remove the stone. Sprinkle with a little caster sugar and place on the barbecue grill over a low direct heat, until softened and lightly browned.

Cut each round in half again and place in a lightly buttered heatproof dish. Sprinkle with the remaining ingredients.

To make the topping, rub the butter into the flour until it resembles breadcrumbs. Stir in the sugar, baking powder and salt. Add the buttermilk and bring it all together to form a cake-style mixture.

Drop spoonfuls of the topping onto the fruit mixture and spread it out with a couple of forks until it roughly covers the fruit. Mix the demerara sugar, flaked almonds and cinnamon together and sprinkle over the top.

Place the dish into the barbecue (lid on) and cook over a medium indirect heat for around 160°C for 30-40 minutes until the top is browned and the fruit juices are bubbling around the sides.

Serve with ice cream, clotted cream or custard.

||||||||||||||||||||||||||||||||||||||||||||||||||||||

Bourbon Pecan Pie

An adult version of this sweet sticky confection – the Bourbon gives it a lovely flavour and mellows out the sweetness.

1 x 9" pre-baked sweet pastry case

3 eggs – lightly beaten

200 g caster sugar

200 g pourable golden syrup

2 tablespoon melted butter

1 teaspoon vanilla extract

25 ml Bourbon whisky

150 g whole pecan nuts

Preheat oven to 160°C.

In a large bowl, beat together the eggs, sugar, syrup, melted butter, vanilla and Jack Daniel's until well blended. Stir in the pecans.

Pour mixture into the pastry case. Bake for approx 50 minutes or until set.

Leave to cool.

(Tip: whisk a little Honey Bourbon whiskey into some double cream and serve it on the side, to give it an extra kick!)

American Style Pancakes

VARIATIONS

Serve with crispy bacon and fried egg with a generous glug of maple syrup over the top.

Add 150 g fresh or frozen blueberries to the mix for blueberry pancakes. Drizzle with maple syrup and cream cheese frosting.

Add two tablespoons cocoa powder and one tablespoon caster sugar to the mix for chocolate pancakes.

Add one teaspoon ground cinnamon to the mix and top with fresh banana slices, toasted pecans and maple syrup.

Serve them for breakfast, a snack or dessert top them with all sorts or fill them with fruit: however you serve them, this is a great base recipe for these wonderful fluffy little pancakes!

200 g self-raising flour
250 g whole milk
80 g sour cream or buttermilk
1 tablespoon melted butter

1 teaspoon baking powder
1 egg
Oil and butter for cooking

Mix the flour and baking powder together and make a well in the centre. Add the egg, milk and buttermilk or sour cream and beat well until smooth, add the melted butter and beat again to incorporate.

Heat a large non-stick frying pan with a little oil and butter until smoking hot and add large spoonfuls of the batter to form small round pancakes (around 10 cm diameter).

Cook on one side until small bubbles form on the pancake, flip the pancakes over and cook until golden brown.

Sweet Potato Surprise

The surprise comes when you cut these open to reveal an ooey-gooey melty marshmallow inside. So bad but yet so good!

2 large sweet potatoes
50 ml maple syrup
50 g butter
50 g brown sugar

200 g Crunchy Nut Cornflakes – crushed
4 jumbo marshmallows

Bake the sweet potatoes until soft (this can be done in a smoker, oven or microwave).

Allow to cool a little, then peel the skins off and place the flesh in a bowl with the maple syrup, butter and sugar. Mash everything together and leave to cool in the fridge.

When cold, take a large marshmallow and form a quarter of the sweet potato mix around it into a ball. Do the same with the other three marshmallows.

Roll the balls in crushed crunchy nut cornflakes and press into the sweet potato to form a good crust. Allow to set for an hour in the fridge.

Bake the balls on a tray in a pre-heated oven or barbecue set to 150°C for around 30-40 minutes.

Serve hot drizzled with more maple syrup if you wish – goes well with ice cream.

Smoked Berry Crumble

Filling
1 kg bag frozen mixed berries

Zest of one lemon

2 tablespoons Bourbon whiskey *(optional)*

1 teaspoon mixed spice

50 g brown sugar

1 tablespoon cornflour

Crumble Topping
150 g flour

115 g butter

110 g brown sugar

½ teaspoon cinnamon

100 g oats

50 g flaked almonds *(optional)*

Set up your barbecue for indirect cooking at approx. 180°C, with some fruitwood for smoke.

Add all of the filling ingredients in a bowl and mix to combine.

To make the crumble, place the flour, cinnamon and butter into a bowl and rub together with your fingertips until it forms a breadcrumb like consistency (do not over-mix). Add the sugar, oats and flaked almonds (if using), mix together.

Butter a heatproof dish or pan and pour the fruit filling in. Scatter the crumble on top.

Place the dish or pan into your barbecue at 180°C and cook for 40-45 minutes or until the fruit is bubbling and the topping has browned lightly.

Serve with ice cream, cream or custard (or a bit of each!).

Chocolate Brownies

Ooey gooey brownies – try using 100 g of your favourite chocolate bar instead of the white and milk chocolate mix (think Snickers or Rolo Brownies)!

185 g butter

185 g dark chocolate

85 g plain flour

40 g cocoa powder

50 g white chocolate

50 g milk chocolate

3 large eggs

275 g caster sugar

75 g chopped walnuts *(optional)*

Set up your barbecue to around 170°C indirect heat (or pre-heat your oven). Line the base of a shallow 20 cm square baking tin.

Put the butter and chocolate into a bowl and place in a microwave for around 60 seconds until melted, stir to mix. Leave the melted mixture to cool.

Whisk the eggs and sugar in a bowl until they look thick and creamy. The mixture should be pale and about double its original volume and should trail a ribbon of mix from the whisk when it is are lifted from the mix.

Pour the cooled chocolate mixture over the egg mixture and whisk again until fully incorporated. Sieve 85 g plain flour and 40 g cocoa powder into the mixture and gently fold in. It will end up looking nice and fudgy. Stop just before you feel you should, as you don't want to overdo this part of the mixing

Chop 50 g white chocolate and 50 g milk chocolate into chunks and stir in until they're dotted throughout. (You can use chocolate chips if you prefer.) Stir in the chopped walnuts if using.

Pour the mixture into the prepared tin. Gently spread the mixture into the corners of the tin and smooth the top with a spatula.

Put in the barbecue (or oven) and cook for 25 mins. Check after 25 minutes by gently shaking the tin; if the brownie wobbles in the middle, it's not quite done, so continue to bake for another 5 minutes until the top has a shiny, papery crust and the sides are just beginning to come away from the tin. Take out of the barbecue (or oven). Leave the whole thing in the tin until cold, then, cut into squares or triangles.

These brownies will keep in an airtight container for a week and in the freezer for up to a month.

Loaded S'mores Bars

These simple little ooey-gooey delights are great after a barbecue, or any time.

120 g butter

1 large egg

200 g brown sugar

100 g plain flour

250 g dark chocolate digestive biscuits *(or biscuits of your choice)* – roughly broken

100 g white chocolate chips

100 g milk chocolate chips

100 g dark chocolate chips

100 g mini marshmallows

Set up barbecue to indirect heat around 175°C in temperature. Line an 8 x 8 inch baking pan with buttered parchment paper.

Melt the butter and allow to cool slightly. Whisk egg, brown sugar and vanilla together before adding the cooled butter. Add the flour and mix until just combined (don't over-mix). Stir in the chopped digestive biscuits, marshmallows and chocolate chips.

Pour the batter into the prepared baking pan, smoothing the top lightly and bake for around 20–30 minutes or until it has firmed up in the centre (the edges will be set).

Allow to cool in the pan for at least 30 minutes before cutting up into bars and serving.

Apple Crumble Muffins

I love these muffins, they always go down well with everyone, especially when I serve them at my Barbecue School with morning coffee!

250 g plain flour

1 teaspoon baking powder

½ teaspoon bicarbonate of soda

½ teaspoon salt

200 g butter

200 g white sugar

3 medium eggs

1 teaspoon vanilla extract

Grated zest of one lemon

1 teaspoon ground cinnamon

½ teaspoon ground nutmeg

Crumble Topping

125 g demerara sugar

60 g plain flour

1 teaspoon ground cinnamon

40 g butter

Preheat oven to 190°C (fan oven 170°C). Line a 12-cup muffin pan with muffin papers.

In a medium bowl, sieve flour, cinnamon, nutmeg, baking powder, bicarbonate of soda and salt. In a large bowl, beat together butter, sugar and eggs until smooth. Mix in vanilla. Stir in apples, and gradually blend in the flour mixture (it should be a fairly stiff mix). Spoon the mixture into the prepared muffin pan. In a small bowl, mix brown sugar, flour and cinnamon. Rub in butter until mixture is like coarse crumbs. Sprinkle over tops of mixture in muffin pan.

Bake for 30 minutes or until a toothpick inserted in the centre of a muffin comes out clean. Allow to sit for 5 minutes before removing muffins from pan. Cool on a wire rack.

Doughnuts

It might sound strange to use dried potato flakes, but I have found that this gives the doughnuts a creamier structure and flavour. I made hundreds of these for the ex-pat community when I lived in Sharm el Sheikh, they made me a very popular person!

350 g plain flour	2 tablespoons vegetable oil
2 teaspoons dry active yeast	75 g dried potato flakes
75 g caster sugar	250 ml warm milk
½ teaspoon salt	

Mix the flour, yeast, sugar, potato flakes and salt into a bowl. Make a well in the entre and add the warm milk and vegetable oil. Mix to a dough and knead until smooth and elastic.

Place in a lightly oiled bowl and leave to rise in a warm place for around an hour. It should double in size.

Knock back the air and remove from the bowl. Knead lightly again and divide into eight pieces. Shape into round balls and leave on a floured surface until risen again.

Heat oil in a large pan to 175°C. (I prefer to use a wok for this.)

Gently drop the doughnuts into the oil and deep fry for 2–3 minutes before flipping over and cooking for a further 2–3 minutes until they are a dark golden colour on both sides.

Remove from the oil and transfer to a large bowl or bag of caster sugar. Coat in the sugar and place on a rack until all the doughnuts are cooked.

Whilst still hot, fill with warm jam or any filling of your choice. (Lemon curd also works well.)

||||||||||||||||||||||||||||||||||||||||||||||||||||||||||||

Lemony Doughnut Twists

A twist on a doughnut shape (excuse the pun) a laminated lemon dough covered in lemon drizzle icing, what's not to like?

300 g strong white flour	Zest of two lemons
1 teaspoon dry active yeast	120 ml lukewarm milk
1 large egg	60 ml lukewarm water
1 teaspoon salt	*Icing*
2 tablespoons vegetable oil	150 g icing sugar – sieved
65 g butter – cubed	Juice of one lemon

Mix the flour, yeast, sugar, cubed butter, lemon zest and salt into a bowl. Make a well in the centre and add the milk, water and egg. Mix to a dough and knead until smooth and elastic. Place in a lightly oiled bowl and leave to rise in a warm place for around an hour. It should double in size.

Remove the dough from the bowl, roll into a rectangle and fold the bottom third up and the top third down. Make a quarter turn, roll out into a rectangle again and repeat the process three more times – the butter lumps should disappear.

Roll into a rectangle around 1 cm thick and cut into strips, fold in the middle and twist twice. Push the ends together to stick them.

Heat oil in a large pan to 170°C (I prefer a wok for this). Gently drop the twists into the oil three or four at a time and deep fry for 2–3 minutes before flipping over and cooking for a further 2–3 minutes until they are a dark golden colour on both sides. Remove from the oil and cool on a rack.

Sieve the icing sugar into a bowl and add enough lemon juice to make a runny icing. Once the twists are cool, dip them into the icing to coat them on all sides.

Place on the rack until the icing has set.

||||||||||||||||||||||||||||||||||||||||||||||||||

Belgian Buns

This is my idea of comfort food. I absolutely love Belgian Buns: sweet, sticky and fruity, cinnamon buns at their best.

Dough
500 g strong plain flour
90 g butter – melted
200 ml lukewarm milk
90 g sugar
2 teaspoons dried active yeast
2 eggs

Filling
30 g butter – melted
30 g sugar
2 teaspoons cinnamon
100 g dried fruit

Decoration
250 g icing sugar
Water
Glace cherries

Place the flour into a large bowl and make a well in the centre. Mix the dried yeast with the milk. Pour the butter and milk into the centre and mix until you get a soft dough. Knead the dough until smooth and elastic and place in a covered bowl in a warm place to prove.

When the dough has doubled in size, knock back. Roll into a rectangle, approx. 40 x 30 cm.

Brush with 30 g melted butter, sprinkle with sugar, cinnamon and fruit, ensuring that the dough is evenly covered with the filling with a 2 cm edge on the long side.

Roll tightly from the longer side and cut into 2.5 cm slices, arrange on a greased tray. Cover with oiled cling film and leave in a warm place until the buns have doubled in size.

Bake in a pre-heated oven at 180°C for 20 minutes until golden brown. Leave to cool on a wire rack.

When cold, make the icing and ice each bun, finishing with half a glacé cherry on top.

> *Variation: try using some lemon curd and sultanas as the filling instead of sugar and cinnamon.*

Carrot Cupcakes with Maple Buttercream Frosting

Your own personal carrot cake, great with a nice cup of tea. Definitely works as one of your five a day!

175 g soft brown sugar
175 ml sunflower oil
3 large eggs
150 g plain flour
1½ teaspoons bicarb of soda
1½ teaspoons baking powder
1 teaspoon cinnamon
½ teaspoon nutmeg

Pinch salt
225 g grated carrot
50 g raisins or sultanas
50 g pecans

Topping
75 g butter
150 g icing sugar
Maple syrup
Pecan halves

In a large bowl, whisk the oil and sugar together until thick. Add the eggs and whisk again. Fold in the fruit, carrots and remaining dry ingredients and mix until fully incorporated.

Pour into cupcake papers until ¾ full. Bake at 170°C for 20–30 minutes, until a skewer inserted comes out clean.

To make the topping, whisk the butter and maple syrup together until soft, add the sieved icing sugar and continue to whisk until light and fluffy. Ice a swirl on top of each cooled cake and top with half a pecan nut.

||||||||||||||||||||||||||||||||||||||||||||||||||||

Chocolate Cherry Cupcakes

This, almost brownie-like cake is a great treat any time and is really simple to make.

125 g soft butter
100 g dark chocolate
300 g good quality cherry jam
100 g sugar
pinch of salt

2 large eggs,
150 g self-raising flour
Icing:
100 g dark chocolate
100 ml double cream

Preheat oven to 180°C.

In a medium size saucepan, over a low heat, melt the butter and chocolate, take the pan off the heat and stir with a wooden spoon until the butter and chocolate are smooth and combined.

Add the jam, sugar, salt and eggs. Stir with a wooden spoon and when is all well combined, stir in the flour.

Pour into cupcake papers and bake at 180°C for 20 minutes, until the cakes have set and a skewer inserted comes out clean.

Cool in the pan on a rack for 10 minutes before placing on a cooling rack.

To make the topping, chop the chocolate into small pieces. Put the cream into a saucepan and bring to the boil. As soon as it reaches boiling point, remove from the heat, add the chocolate and leave for 1 minute before whisking. Leave to cool and whisk again until thick and smooth.

Pipe a swirl on top of each cooled cupcake.

||||||||||||||||||||||||||||||||||||||||||||||||||

Banana and White Chocolate Muffins

175 g butter or margarine

225 g light brown sugar

350 g self-raising flour

3 eggs

3 large or 4 medium, very ripe bananas

100 g white chocolate chunks

Extra melted white chocolate for topping (optional)

Heat the oven to 180°C. Mash the bananas. Cream the butter and sugar together and beat in the bananas, then the eggs. Fold in the flour. Put the mixture into cupcake papers in a muffin pan and bake for 20 minutes or until a skewer comes out clean. Drizzle melted white chocolate over the top if desired.

Lemonylicious Cupcakes

Lovely little lemon cakes, simple and delicious. (Also works with orange or lime.)

175 g butter

175 g caster sugar

3 large eggs

175 g self-raising flour

Zest of two lemons – finely grated

Juice of one lemon

100 g lemon curd (*see recipe*)

Topping

75 g butter

200 g icing sugar

Zest and juice of one lemon

In a large bowl, whisk the butter and sugar together until fluffy. Whisk in the eggs, lemon juice and zest before folding in the flour. Spoon into cupcake papers until ¾ full. Bake at 170°C for 20–30 minutes, until a skewer inserted comes out clean. While the cakes are still warm, inject some lemon curd into the centre of each cake.

To make the topping, whisk the butter, lemon juice and zest together until soft, add the sieved icing sugar and continue to whisk until light and fluffy. Ice a swirl on top of each cooled cake.

Old Fashioned Almond Macaroons

These simple macaroons are a family favourite. They have a lovely chewy texture beneath a crisp surface.

4 egg whites

175 g caster sugar

225 g ground almonds

1 teaspoon almond extract

12 whole almonds to decorate

Mix sugar and ground almonds in a bowl. Beat egg whites until foamy and slightly fluffy, add the almond extract.

Gradually, add the sugar and ground almonds to the egg white mixture until a soft dough is formed.

Roll into 1–1½ inch balls and place onto a greased baking sheet. *(Hint: use a small ice cream scoop to get perfect rounds.)* Dip three fingers into water and flatten each ball slightly. Press a whole unblanched almond onto the top of each one.

Bake at 180˚C or gas mark 4 for 15–20 minutes until light golden in colour. Allow to cool for 5 minutes on the baking sheet before transferring to a cooling rack.

Choc 'n' Nut Cookies

This is my go-to recipe for cookies. I change the chocolate and nuts depending on what's in my cupboard. Always good for a treat.

75 g butter

75 g white sugar

75 g brown sugar

1 egg

Few drops of vanilla extract

175 g self-raising flour

100 g chocolate chips or chunks

50 g nuts

Cream together butter and sugars; beat in egg and vanilla. Fold in the flour, chocolate and nuts. You should now have a stiff dough.

Use an ice cream scoop to make balls of dough and put onto prepared baking sheets (6 will fill an average baking sheet). Bake at 180°C for 12–13 minutes until pale golden in colour (this will give a chewy cookie). For a crunchier cookie, bake for an extra 3 minutes.

Leave on baking sheet to set for a couple of minutes before moving to a cooling rack.

VARIATIONS

I've made these cookies with chocolate chunks, white, dark, milk or a mix. Macadamia nuts, pistachios or hazelnuts go really well too.

Cranberry, Oatmeal and White Chocolate Cookies

125 g butter
150 g soft brown sugar
1 egg
150 g jumbo oats
150 g self-raising flour
1 teaspoon cinnamon

1 teaspoon vanilla extract
½ teaspoon salt
150 g dried cranberries
100 g white chocolate chips

Set your oven or barbecue to 170°C… Cream together butter and sugar…add egg, vanilla and mix. Add oats, cinnamon, flour, baking powder and bicarbonate…mix well. Add white chocolate chips to the mix with dried cranberries. Drop spoonfuls of the mix onto baking sheet. (I use parchment paper over the sheet, or just butter the sheet to stop them sticking.)

Bake for around 13 minutes until golden. Remove from oven. Leave the cookies on the baking sheet to set for 10 minutes before transferring to the cooling rack.

||||||||||||||||||||||||||||||||||||||||||||||

Whiskey-Soaked Dundee Cake

This is a really good fruitcake for those who don't like heavy, rich fruitcake. It does have an excellent flavour and a light crumbly texture. It's also Dave's favourite cake.

200 g butter
200 g light brown sugar
4 large eggs
325 g plain flour
1½ teaspoons baking powder
milk, if needed
200 g raisins
200 g sultanas
125 g glacé cherries, cut into halves

3 level tablespoons ground almonds
Grated zest of one orange and one lemon
5 tablespoons whisky *(or strong tea, if you must)*
Blanched almonds and halved glacé cherries to decorate

The night before… Put raisins and sultanas into a bowl and pour the whisky (or tea) over so that the fruit plumps up. Cover and leave in a warm place.

Pre-heat the oven to 170°C.

Put the butter and sugar in a mixing bowl and beat until light and fluffy. Whisk the eggs one at a time into the creamed butter and sugar. *(Tip: putting in a tablespoon of the pre-weighed flour after each egg will stop the cake mix from curdling.)* Fold in the remaining flour and baking powder. The mixture needs to be of a soft, dropping consistency; if it seems dry, add a little milk to loosen the mixture. Fold in the raisins, sultanas, cherries, ground almonds, orange and lemon zests.

Spoon the mixture into a lined 20 cm cake tin, smoothing it out evenly. Arrange the almonds and cherries in circles on top of the mixture. Do this carefully and lightly: if they are pressed in, they will sink during baking. Place the cake in the centre of the oven and bake for 1½ to 2 hours or until the centre is firm and springy to the touch and a skewer inserted into the cake comes out clean. Let the cake cool completely before removing it from the tin.

This cake keeps very well in an airtight tin and tastes even better if kept for a few days before cutting.

Figola (Maltese Easter Biscuits)

I found this recipe handwritten in the back of one of my old cookbooks. The recipe has been passed down from my Maltese grandfather. It makes a lovely change to an Easter Egg!

Biscuit Dough
225 g caster sugar
120 g butter
2 large eggs
Grated rind of one lemon
450 g plain flour
Milk if needed

Filling
170 g caster sugar
120 g ground almonds
Grated rind of one lemon
Whites of two small eggs

Topping
Icing sugar
Lemon juice

To make the biscuit dough, cream together the butter, sugar and lemon zest, beat in the eggs. Add the flour to make a soft dough (add a little milk if needed).

To make the filling, whisk the egg whites until frothy, add the other ingredients and mix to a wet dough consistency.

Roll out the biscuit dough and cut into shapes of your choice: you will need two of each shape. Fill each biscuit with a thin layer of the filling, leaving a small edge. Dampen the edge slightly with water and place the second biscuit on top, sealing the edges to enclose the filling. Place on a line baking tray and bake in a preheated oven at 180°C for around 20–30 minutes until the biscuits are golden brown.

Mix the sieved icing sugar with some lemon juice to a fairly thick consistency. Leave to cool and decorate with the lemon icing (hopefully not as badly as mine)!

Sticky Toffee Cake with Salted Caramel Buttercream

I was asked to come up with a recipe for this as a tier in a family Wedding Cake I was making. The topping isn't what made it to the cake but works so well!

Cake
380 g pitted dates
250 ml water
2 teaspoons bicarbonate of soda
200 g butter
250 g light muscovado sugar
4 large eggs
30 g maple syrup
2 teaspoons vanilla extract
350 g self-raising flour

Icing/Filling
200 g butter
400 g icing sugar
120 g dulce de leche *(I used Nestlé's Carnation Caramel)*
10 g sea salt flakes

Topping
2 chocolate fudge fingers
100 g dulce de leche *(or the remainder of the can)*
2 tablespoons rum *(optional)*

Preheat the oven to 175°C and line 2 x 20 cm round cake tins with non-stick baking parchment. Butter the sides of the tin.

Place the dates and water in a small saucepan and bring to the boil. Remove from the heat. Add two teaspoons of bicarbonate of soda and stir well and quickly. Blend the date mixture into a thick purée.

Melt the butter and leave to cool. Place the eggs, sugar, vanilla extract and maple syrup into a large bowl and whisk until thick and creamy. Slowly, add the melted butter whilst whisking. Mix in the dates until fully incorporated. Gently, fold in the flour until you have a nice smooth cake mix.

Divide the mix between the two cake tins, level out the tops and place in the pre-heated oven for around 35 minutes or until a skewer inserted into the cake comes out clean.

Remove from the oven and leave in the tins for around 10 minutes before removing and cooling on a cooling rack.

To make the buttercream, whisk the softened butter together with the dulce de leche, gradually add the sieved icing sugar and whisk together until soft and fluffy. Stir in the sea salt flakes and set the mix aside while the cake cools.

Mix the remaining dulce de leche with the rum over a low heat until smooth.

To assemble the cake, sandwich the cake with half of the buttercream mix and either spread or pipe the remainder on the top of the cake. Drizzle the dulce de leche and rum mix over the top of the cake, allowing it to drip down the sides and sprinkle the chopped-up fudge pieces on top.

Chocolate Cake with Smoked Chocolate Ganache Frosting

A rich but light chocolate cake.

Cake
350 g self-raising flour

4 tablespoon cocoa powder

2 teaspoons bicarbonate soda

300 g caster sugar

4 eggs beaten

300 ml *(½ pint)* sunflower oil

300 ml *(½ pint)* semi skimmed milk

4 tablespoons golden syrup

Coating and filling
200 g dark chocolate

200 g milk chocolate

400 ml double cream

50 g butter

Pinch of salt

Pre-heat oven to 180°C/350°F/Gas Mark 4. Grease and line two 20 cm (8 inch) sandwich tins.

Sieve the flour, cocoa and bicarbonate of soda into a bowl. Add the sugar and mix well.

Make a well in the centre and add the syrup, eggs, oil and milk. Beat well with electric whisk until smooth.

Spoon the mixture into the two tins and bake for 30–35 minutes until risen and firm to the touch. Remove from oven, leave to cool slightly before turning out onto a cooling rack.

To make the Smoked Chocolate Ganache:

Slowly and gently, melt the butter and chocolate together in a bowl in the smoker set to 125°C, stirring occasionally until thick and glossy. Do not allow it to smoke for too long as it will become bitter. Mix in the slightly warmed cream and whisk gently until creamy.

Allow the ganache to cool slightly, stirring occasionally to stop a crust forming. Use a third to sandwich your cake together and two-thirds for the topping and sides.

Chocolate Cheesecake brownies

Cheesecake and brownies: the ultimate sweet combination.

Brownie Mix
225 g dark chocolate (minimum 52% cocoa solids)
150 g unsalted butter
3 large eggs
225 g caster sugar
100 ml strong espresso coffee
100 g plain flour

Cheesecake Swirl
150 g full fat cream cheese
50 g caster sugar
1 large egg
Zest of ½ orange

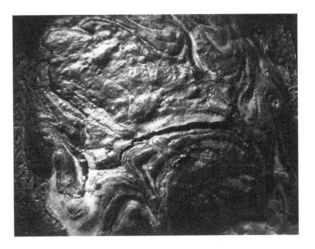

Preheat the oven to 170°C. Grease and line a 20 cm square cake tin.

To make the brownies, melt the chocolate and butter in a bowl set over a pan of simmering water. (Do not let the base of the bowl touch the water.) Remove the bowl from the pan and set aside to cool slightly.

Whisk the eggs, caster sugar and coffee in a bowl until well combined. Sift in the flour and mix until well combined.

To make the cheesecake, beat the cream cheese, caster sugar, egg and orange zest until smooth.

Spoon the brownie mixture into the cake tin then spoon the cheesecake mixture on top and use a knife to cut lines into the mixture to create a marble effect.

Bake in the oven for 25–30 minutes, or until just set. Remove the tin from the oven, leave to cool in the tin and then cut into squares.

Chocolate Stout Cake with Raspberries

This rich chocolate cake with its shiny mirror glaze is a real centrepiece. It has bursts of fresh raspberry and is a wonderful dessert or teatime treat.

Cake
325 ml chocolate stout
100 ml espresso coffee
460 g unsalted butter
150 g cocoa powder (unsweetened)
675 g plain flour
800 g caster sugar
1 tablespoon bicarbonate of soda
1 teaspoon salt
4 large eggs
330 ml buttermilk
1 tablespoon vanilla extract

Filling
200 g 52% chocolate
200 ml double cream
200 g fresh raspberries

Crumb Coating
100 g unsalted butter
200 g icing sugar
Zest and juice of two oranges

Mirror Glaze
4 sheets gelatine
125 ml water
225 g granulated sugar
150 g 52% Chocolate
30 g cocoa powder
65 ml double cream

Cake – Pre-heat oven to 160°C. Butter the sides and line the bases of 3 x 20 cm cake pans.

Place the stout, coffee and butter in a saucepan and bring to a simmer until the butter has melted. Sieve in the cocoa powder and whisk until fully incorporated. Leave to cool.

Sieve the flour into a bowl with the sugar, salt and bicarbonate of soda and mix.

In a large bowl, whisk the eggs, vanilla and buttermilk together until smooth. Add the cooled chocolate stout mixture to the egg mix and whisk until fully incorporated. Add the flour and sugar mixture and fold in until you have a smooth batter.

Divide the batter equally between the three cake pans and place in the pre-heated oven. Bake for approximately 50–60 minutes until a skewer inserted into the centre of the cake comes out almost clean.

Cool in the pans for around 10 minutes, before turning out onto cooling racks to cool completely.

Filling – Break up the chocolate and place into a bowl, place the double cream in a saucepan and bring almost to the boil. Pour the cream over the chocolate and leave for a couple of minutes before mixing well until smooth. Leave to cool, stirring often, until thick and spreadable.

Crumb Coating – Place the butter, orange zest and juice into a large bowl and whisk until soft and fluffy. Add the sieved icing sugar gradually and mix into a firm buttercream.

Mirror Glaze – Soak four sheets of gelatine in cold water.

In a small pan, boil the water and sugar together until the mixture reaches 104°C, then remove from the heat. Add the broken-up chocolate and mix well, add the sieved cocoa powder and mix in, add the double cream and hand whisk the whole mixture until it is smooth.

Squeeze out the gelatine sheets and add to the mixture, whisk until fully melted and pour the mixture through a sieve into a jug and using a stick blender, blend until smooth. Pour mixture through a sieve into a new jug and leave to cool to a maximum of 29°C, stirring often.

Assembling the Cake – Trim the cakes until they are flat and level. Place the bottom layer of the cake onto a thin 20 cm cake board. Spread half of the filling over the bottom layer and top with halved raspberries, spread a little of the buttercream coating on the base of the next cake and place on top of the raspberries. Repeat the process with the next layer.

Using the remaining buttercream, apply a smooth coating to the top and sides of the cake, place in the fridge to set.

Once the cake is nice and cold and the mirror glaze has cooled to 29°C, take the cake and sit it on an upturned bowl over a large pan (this will catch the excess mirror glaze). Slowly, pour the glaze over the top and sides of the cake until it is fully coated. Scrape off the excess glaze from the very bottom of the cake and place the cake on a larger cake board (I quite like using a square board). Place in the fridge until set.

To Serve – You really don't want to serve big slabs of cake as it is very rich. This cake should easily serve 20 people. If serving as a dessert, you could serve with ice cream or cream and more fresh raspberries.

Bagels

500 g of bread flour or high gluten flour (*plus extra for kneading*)

2 teaspoons of active dry yeast

1½ tablespoons of granulated sugar

325 ml of warm water (*you may need a little more or less*)

1½ teaspoons of salt

Mix the flour and salt, yeast and sugar in a large bowl. Make a well in the middle and pour in 250 ml of warm water. Mix and stir in the rest of the water as needed. Depending on where you live, you may need to add anywhere from a couple tablespoons to about ¼ cup of water. You want to result in a moist and firm dough after you have mixed it. On a floured countertop, knead the dough for about 10 minutes until it is smooth and elastic. Lightly oil a large bowl and place the dough in it. Cover the bowl with a damp dishtowel. Let rise in a warm place for 1 hour, until the dough has doubled in size. Punch the air out of the dough and let it rest for another 10 minutes.

Divide the dough into eight pieces. Shape each piece into a round roll, coat your index finger in flour and gently press it into the centre of each dough ball to form a ring. Stretch the ring to about one-third of the diameter of the bagel and place on a lightly oiled baking sheet. Repeat the same step with the remaining dough. After shaping the dough rounds and placing them on the baking sheet, cover with a damp cloth or oiled cling film and allow to rest until doubled in size. Meanwhile, preheat your oven to 200°C.

Bring a large pot of water to a boil (I prefer using a wok for this). Reduce the heat. Gently pick up the bagels and lower them into the water simmer for one minute before flipping them over and simmering for another minute (you can increase this to two minutes if you want a chewier bagel). Remove from the water and place back on the baking sheet.

Bake for 20–30 minutes, until golden brown.

Brioche Style Burger/ Hotdog Buns

Fad or not, I like the texture of a good brioche bun with my burger, I'm not keen on sweet buns so reduced the sugar in this recipe.

200 ml water

100 ml milk

75 g butter

500 g + 50 g bread flour

10 g active dry yeast

15 g caster sugar

1½ teaspoons salt

2 large eggs, beaten

1 egg yolk, beaten with two tablespoons water, for egg wash

Sesame seeds (*optional*)

Melt the butter into the milk and combine with the water. In a large bowl (or food mixer with a dough hook) combine 550 g of the flour, the yeast, salt and sugar. Add the warm liquid and the beaten eggs and mix until incorporated. Add the remaining flour a couple of tablespoons at a time whilst mixing until the dough comes away from the side of the bowl and is still slightly sticky to the touch. Knead until smooth; you should be able to stretch the dough without it breaking. Place the dough in a lightly floured bowl. Cover with cling film and leave in a warm place to rise until doubled in size.

Knock back the dough and allow to rest for a few minutes. Divide into 10–12 equal pieces and shape into balls or fingers make them around half the size of the burger or sausage as they will double in size. Place on a buttered baking tray, brush some cling film with melted butter and place loosely over the buns. Leave in a warm place to rise for 30 minutes to 1 hour.

When ready to bake, preheat oven to 190°C. Brush buns with egg wash and sprinkle with sesame seeds (optional).

Bake until golden brown, about 12-14 minutes. Cool completely on a wire rack.

||||||||||||||||||||||||||||||||||||||||||||||||||

Cheese Pretzels

Dough
500 g strong white flour

130 ml *(approx.)* warm water

75 g grated cheese

2 teaspoons active dry yeast

1 egg

1 teaspoon sea salt

2 teaspoons sugar

½ teaspoon cayenne powder

½ teaspoon granulated garlic

Filling and Glaze
200 g grated cheese

1 egg

2 tablespoons milk

1 teaspoon poppy seeds

Preheat the oven to 200°C.

Mix together the warm water and the yeast. Stir and let sit for 10 minutes. Add the dry ingredients from the dough mix into a large bowl along with 1 egg and the warm water and yeast mixture. Mix until the dough comes together. Turn out onto a lightly floured work surface and knead until the dough is smooth and elastic, adding a little flour if it gets sticky.

Roll out the dough to a large rectangle, about ½ cm thick. Sprinkle half of the Cheddar in the middle (short way). Fold a third of the dough over and sprinkle with the remaining Cheddar. Fold the last third over and pinch the edges closed. Roll with a rolling pin to form a large rectangle. Cut into 3 cm lengthwise strips.

Pinch the cut edges together and then roll into a cigar shape. Form into a pretzel shape and put on a baking sheet lined with a silicone baking mat.

Beat the remaining egg and the milk in a small bowl. Mix well. Brush the formed pretzels with the egg mixture and then sprinkle evenly with the poppy seeds (you could also use sesame seeds, onion flakes or flaked salt).

Bake until golden brown, about 15 to 18 minutes. Remove from the oven and let cool. Serve warm or at room temperature.

Printed in the USA
CPSIA information can be obtained
at www.ICGtesting.com
LVHW070705290823
756539LV00006B/38